W9-BNP-412

Gladiators

BEN HUBBARD

Cavendish
Square

New York

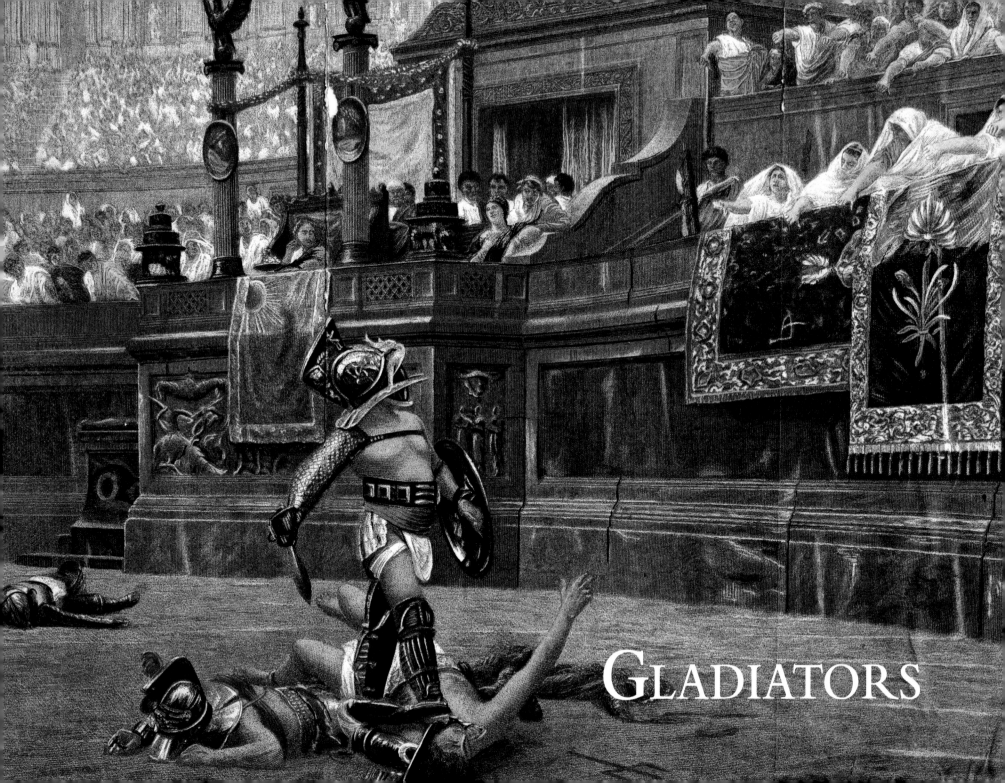

GLADIATORS

Published in 2017 by Cavendish Square Publishing, LLC
243 5th Avenue, Suite 136, New York, NY 10016

First Edition

Website: cavendishsq.com

This publication represents the opinions and views of the author based on his or her personal experience, knowledge, and research. The information in this book serves as a general guide only. The author and publisher have used their best efforts in preparing this book and disclaim liability rising directly or indirectly from the use and application of this book.

CPSIA Compliance Information: Batch #CW17CSQ

All websites were available and accurate when this book was sent to press.

Cataloging-in-Publication Data

Names: Hubbard, Ben.
Title: Gladiators / Ben Hubbard.
Description: New York : Cavendish Square, 2017. | Series: Conquerors and combatants | Includes index.
Identifiers: ISBN 9781502624574 (library bound) | ISBN 9781502624581 (ebook)
Subjects: LCSH: Gladiators--Rome--History--Juvenile literature.
Classification: LCC GV35.H83 2017 | DDC 937--dc23

Editorial Director: David McNamara
Editor: Renni Johnson
Associate Art Director: Amy Greenan
Production Coordinator: Karol Szymczuk

Printed in the United States of America

Contents

Introduction

The gladiatorial games lay at the center of Roman life. Citizens flocked to their local amphitheater to be entertained by animal hunts, public executions and gladiators fighting to the death. Thousands died during large and lavish games that sometimes lasted for weeks on end. However, these festivals of killing were not unusual for those attending—it was simply a part of being Roman. The history of the gladiators is inextricably linked with the story of Rome and its emperors. At the peak of Rome's imperial age, emperors provided games on an increasingly extravagant scale. They spared no expense in entertaining the public and showing off Rome's power and dominion over man and beast.

The Spectacle of Death

Exotic animals such as elephants, crocodiles, and rhinoceroses were imported from foreign shores to be slaughtered in front of the crowd. In the amphitheater, harmless herbivores were let loose among large forest sets before being hunted down and killed en masse.

Other more dangerous animals such as bulls and bears were chained together and forced to fight. Men with spears dispatched panthers, lions, and tigers and were, in turn, often torn apart by these dangerous predators. Wild animals were also set onto enemies of state, who were sometimes nailed upside down to a cross. Others were also crucified after first being dressed in tunics covered with pitch; after being nailed to the cross they were set alight. Thousands of Christians executed in this way were used as human torches to illuminate the games held by Emperor Nero. Nero was a great supporter of the gladiatorial spectacles and fond of inventing storylines for the public executions. On one occasion he dressed a man like the mythological figure Daedalus and flew him across the arena on wires to be devoured by bears. Nero even entered the arena himself, sometimes dressing in the skin of a wild animal and attacking men and women tied to stakes.

Other emperors also had an appetite for the blood of the amphitheater: Claudius liked watching the expressions of gladiators as they died; Caligula enjoyed forcing the sick, elderly, and disabled to fight to the death. Commodus actually fought in the Colosseum as a gladiator. The emperor

Above: A third-century-BCE funerary relief created by "Ammias of Araxios," in memory of her husband, a gladiator.

Facing page: The animal hunts or *venationes*, shown in this relief, made up the morning event of a gladiatorial spectacle.

Above: An emperor's participation at a gladiatorial spectacle was an important part of his relationship with his people. Many got it wrong.

Commodus's antics in the arena made him a laughing stock with the public and the Roman Senate. The games were an emperor's gift to his people, but they were also a time when he had to judge his participation carefully. A clever emperor would enjoy the games as an enthusiastic spectator but also maintain his royal dignity. Tiberius got it wrong by not showing up to the games at all; Commodus, on the other hand, took it too far. He sealed his ignominious end by announcing he would inaugurate the year 193 CE dressed as a gladiator.

Plebeians and Patricians

The games were attended by both rich and poor and the amphitheater was a microcosm of Roman society: wealthy citizens known as patricians sat nearest the arena floor, dressed in white togas; other, lesser citizens called Plebeians sat above them in their colorful tunics. The amphitheater was a great amplifier of public opinion and ordinary Romans, feeling protected within the crowd, often voiced their displeasure at the emperor. This had to be done carefully, as some emperors were known to bristle at criticism and then become vindictive. Caligula once remarked he wished the Colosseum crowd had a single neck so he could kill it at one blow; Domitian threw a spectator to the dogs after he badmouthed a *murmillo*, his favorite type of gladiator.

Astute emperors gave the people what they wanted. Titus had wooden balls thrown into the crowd at the day's end, each one representing a gift to be collected. More commonly, emperors curried favor with the spectators by obeying their wishes

dressed in the skin of a lion, carried a club and likened himself to the mythical demigod Hercules. He also called himself one of the greatest gladiators who had ever lived.

However, his bouts in the arena were a farce, as both the emperor and his opponent were only ever armed with wooden swords. It was only behind his closed palace doors that Commodus used a steel blade, where he often cut the noses and ears off his sparring partners while practicing his swordplay.

to let a defeated gladiator live or be killed. This occurred at the end of a bout where one gladiator had been beaten, lost his weaponry, or was too injured to go on. At this time he would hold his index finger up in submission. His opponent would then look to the crowd questioningly: "Should I kill him, or not?" This was the spectators' cue to make their feelings clear. By sticking out their hands and turning their thumbs they would indicate whether the defeated man should be finished off or granted a *missio*, a reprieve. emperors wanting to please the crowd followed their lead. Others, who included both Caligula and Domitian, showed their antipathy for their people by going against them.

Defeated gladiators who had fought bravely

Right: Gladiators included prisoners of war, condemned criminals, and disobedient slaves, who were clapped in chains and transported to a gladiator school.

Below: Much of what we know about the gladiators comes from mosaics in Roman villas such as this one from Negrar, in modern Verona.

and won the respect of the crowd were often allowed to live. Every gladiator was expected to fight according to the virtues that had made Rome great, including training (*disciplina*), contempt for death (*contemptus mortis*), love of glory (*amor laudis*), and the desire to win (*cupido victoriae*). However, those defeated gladiators who had not been granted a *missio* were still expected to die honorably. They would do so by wrapping their arms around their opponent's legs and waiting for the fatal sword thrust between their shoulder blades.

Power and Glory

The virtues that Rome demanded of its gladiators were those displayed by its legionaries, who, under the command of ambitious generals, conquered two-thirds of the ancient world. Rome's invasions of Sicily, Carthage, and the countries of the western Mediterranean set it on its path to becoming the greatest power the world had ever known. Riches plundered from these new territories were sent back to Rome by the wagonload.

Alongside the tons of gold, silver, and bronze entering Rome were vast numbers of slaves and prisoners of war. The armaments of these conquered tribal warriors such as the Gauls and Thracians were styled into the first types of gladiators. This gave the public the chance to see in the arena the

enemies of Rome who had been overcome on the battlefield. Many foreign warriors who had fought against Rome ended up being sentenced to a gladiator school. They were now the *infamis*—the disgraced, lower on the social ladder than actors and prostitutes. Their only chance of survival was to train hard and beat every opponent in the arena. Only the greatest and best-loved gladiators were awarded the wooden *rudis*, the symbol of their freedom, and allowed to leave the arena forever.

As Rome grew into a large empire, its elite families became wealthier from the spoils of war than they could ever have imagined. Many grabbed huge tracts of land, pushing Roman farmers out and making their new slaves work the soil. As corrupt senators feathered their nests and ordinary Romans became destitute, a new brand of military "hard man" seized control. These were the men still well known to us in the modern age: Sulla, Pompey, Caesar. Each of these ruthless generals cared little for the democratic machinations of the Senate or the ideological pretentions of the Roman Republic. Instead they wanted power and the creation of a legacy that would make their names live forever.

Bread and Circuses

Julius Caesar knew the best way to achieve control was to win over the Roman public. He did so by providing the most grandiose gladiatorial games the ancient world had ever seen. He gave gifts of money and grain to the people of Rome, bankrupting himself in the process and borrowing heavily against his future successes. It was a political masterstroke, one that earned Caesar the love and adulation of the public and sparked the poet's phrase that still lives on 2,000 years later—*panem et circenses*, bread and circuses.

With his policy of bread and circuses, Caesar created the blueprint of rule for every Roman leader who followed him. Caesar, of course, did not survive long enough to witness the full success of his policy: the Senate, fearing the general had become a tyrant, stabbed him to death during a senatorial meeting. But Caesar's heir and successor, Augustus, adopted bread and circuses to the letter, becoming Rome's first and greatest emperor in the process.

Under Augustus, Rome grew into an empire that would control 1.9 million square miles (5 million square kilometers) of land and rule 60 million subjects. Rome's success was due to its determined and pragmatic approach to expansion. It turned every new conquered territory into a smaller version of Rome. A Roman infrastructure was then added to every new town and city: aqueducts to supply fresh water, public baths to keep its inhabitants clean, and an amphitheater for the gladiatorial entertainment. Provincial elites were employed to collect taxes and keep the local population in line by copying the bread and circuses program developed in the capital. This system of Roman rule was known as the *pax*

Above: The success of Roman civilization was based on the brilliance of its engineering works. Many of the aqueducts, which brought clean water to all Roman citizens, still stand today.

Facing page: A romantic rendering shows the *Forum Romanum*, the center of Rome and the setting for early *munera*.

Above: Every Roman city had public baths, temples, an aqueduct, and an amphitheater for gladiatorial games, such as this one in the ancient city of Segobriga, Cuenca, Spain.

Right: A 2013 gladiatorial reenactment marks the anniversary of the legendary founding of Rome in 753 BCE.

Facing page: A reenactment of a *pompa*, the procession before a gladiatoral contest in the arena.

romana, the Roman peace, which brought its citizens prosperity, protection, and all the trappings of the world's most advanced civilization. Most importantly it gave the people from its conquered territories the chance to become Roman. But in the end, the people of the empire needed something Rome could not supply: spiritual fulfillment.

Rise and Fall of the Empire

In the capital, the debauched and sometimes deranged emperors who succeeded Augustus turned Rome into a metropolis of vice and corruption financed by imperial loot. emperors played out their most depraved fantasies in public and bribed and infantilized the people: the mob was born. Their

imperial games became opulent extravaganzas that lasted for weeks on end and introduced new and novel ways of slaying man and beast. But in the provinces, far from the toxic center of Rome, an unforeseen threat began to take shape. A religious movement, later called Christianity, provided people with spiritual and moral guidance not available under the *pax romana*.

It was this small religious sect from the East that ended up subverting the Roman Empire and aiding its decline and fall. While Christianity rose, the aqueducts, baths, and temples of Rome crumbled as a dark age fell over Europe. Medieval pilgrims traveled to the sites of executed martyrs; decaying amphitheaters were plundered for their marble and overgrown with weeds.

In modern times millions of tourists flock to the Colosseum in Rome. Here, they can try and imagine the lives of thousands of Roman citizens who went to the gladiatorial games for a daylong bill of violence and visceral pleasure. They can gaze into the arena and wonder about those who fought and died there, and the kind of civilization that turned death and torture into a form of entertainment.

Origins

Gladiatorial contests as we know them today—a hand-to-hand duel to the death between armed combatants—became a feature of Roman life from the third century BCE. The exact origins of these contests, however, remain something of a mystery. The only consensus between historians past and present is that the gladiator fights did not originate in Rome.

I n its broadest terms, the gladiatorial tradition is linked to the shedding of blood at the funerals of important people. Human sacrifice as part of a funeral ceremony was not an uncommon occurrence in the early civilizations of the ancient world. When archeologist Leonard Woolley discovered the Mesopotamian city of Ur in 1922, he unearthed the royal tombs known today as the "death pits." Dating from around 2600 BCE, these were sites of mass sacrifice where the royal family was buried with its servants. As the bodies of these servants were discovered in neat lines, Woolley surmised that they had ingested poison before taking up their final prearranged positions.

Facing page: Tomb paintings such as this one found in Paestum, Campania, are among the earliest known representations of gladiators.

Right: A gladiatorial relief depicting a victorious *secutor* adorns the Diocletian baths in Rome.

Human sacrifice at funerals was also a feature of Mediterranean cultures, such as the Mycenaeans of Bronze Age Greece. They believed that blood spilt on the graves of fallen warriors would aid them on their journey to the afterlife. In the *Iliad*, Homer describes Achilles honoring the fallen Patroclus in this way:

> "Then he completed the grim
> task he had in mind, killing
> twelve noble sons of the brave
> Trojans with his bronze blade,
> and setting the pyre alight so
> the pitiless flames would spread.
> Then he gave a groan, and
> called his dear friend by name:
> 'All hail to you, Patroclus,
> though in the House of Hades.
> See how I keep the promises
> I made. Twelve noble sons of

Above: The Royal Tombs of the ancient Sumerian city of Ur, in modern-day Iraq. Ur was the site of human sacrifice as part of funerary ceremonies for nobles.

Facing page: A nineteenth-century artist's impression of the funeral pyre of Patroclus, the fallen hero of the *Iliad*.

brave Trojans, the fire will devour with you. But the dogs, not the flames, shall feed on Hector, son of Priam.'"
—Homer, the *Iliad*, translated by Samuel Butler

Festus, a second-century-CE scholar, suggests that the first gladiator fights were actually developed as a less cruel substitute for the sacrifices carried out on warriors' tombs. This development was

often attributed to the Etruscans, the civilization that borrowed heavily from the Greeks and in turn passed many of its customs on to the Romans. The Etruscans were known to sacrifice prisoners of war on their warriors' tombs, and a line from first-century-BCE Greek writer Nikolaos of Damascus also confirmed their gladiatorial involvement:

"The Romans organized performances by gladiators, a habit they had acquired from

the Etruscans, not only at festivals and in the theaters, but also at feasts. That is to say, certain people would frequently invite their friends for a meal and other pleasant pastimes, but in addition there might be two or three pairs of gladiators. When everyone had had plenty to eat and drink they called for the gladiators. The moment anyone's throat was cut, they clapped their hands in pleasure. And it sometimes even turned out that someone had specified in their will that the most beautiful women he had purchased were to fight each other, or someone else might have set down that two boys, his favorites, were to do so."
—Quoted in Athenaeus's *The Learned Banqueters*, translated by S. Douglas Olson

Funeral Fresco

The theory that Roman gladiators originated with the Etruscans was widely accepted for centuries, despite the lack of any hard evidence to back it up. Notably, there were no convincing depictions of gladiator contests found in Etruscan tomb paintings, traditionally a primary source for archeologists. The closest example was found in a sixth-century-BCE Etruscan tomb in Tarquinia in central Italy. Here, a man is shown being attacked by a wild cat, which is held on a leash by another man. Advocates of the Etruscan theory argued that the painting depicted the animal hunts, which later appeared on the day-long gladiatorial program. But there was still no sign of armed warriors fighting each other, and critics suggested that the link was tenuous at best.

Spectacle or Sport?

As time went on the religious significance of the *munus* as a funeral ceremony was all but forgotten as the event became purely about sport. This, among other issues, was seized upon by the Christian writer Tertullian (160–220 CE) in his condemnation of the gladiatorial games:

"It remains to examine the most famous, the most popular spectacle of all. It is called *munus* (a service) from being a service due … The ancients thought that by this sort of spectacle they rendered a service to the dead, after they had tempered it with a more cultured form of cruelty. For of old, in the belief that the souls of the dead are propitiated with human blood, they used at funerals to sacrifice captives or slaves of poor quality whom they bought. Afterwards it seemed good to obscure their impiety by making it a pleasure. So after the persons procured had been trained in such arms as they then had and as best they might—their training was to learn to be killed!—they then did them to death on the appointed funeral day at the tombs. So they found comfort for death in murder. This is the origin of the *munus*. But by and by they progressed to the same height in refinement as in cruelty; for the pleasure of the holiday lacked something, unless savage beasts too had their share in tearing men's bodies to pieces. What was offered to appease the dead was counted as a funeral rite. This type of thing is idolatry, for idolatry too is a type of funeral rite; the one and the other are alike service to the dead. For in the images of the dead demons have their abode."

—Tertullian, *De Spectaculis*, translated by S. Thelwall

Right: Tertullian's *De Spectaculis* was a moral treatise on Rome's gladiatorial games.

Then, in the mid-twentieth century, the discovery of tomb paintings in Campania, Italy, offered up fresh evidence for the gladiatorial origins debate. A fourth-century-BCE fresco found in the city of Paestum depicted scenes from funeral games that include a chariot race and single combat between two men armed with shields and spears. An official standing beside the fighters indicates it is an organized bout rather than a brawl.

As Campania was first colonized by the Greeks, it may be that the region became responsible for replacing human sacrifice at funerals with mortal combat between two warriors. One point is undisputed—Campania turned into the great hub of gladiatorial activity under Rome; the leading gladiator schools were situated there, as were the first stone amphitheaters. Julius Caesar himself later owned a gladiator school in Capua, Campania.

Facing page: This sixth-century-BCE Etruscan mural discovered in the Tomb of the Auguries, Tarquinia, led to the theory that the gladiatorial contests were of Etruscan origin.

MUNERA

The first Roman gladiator contests took place at the funerals of rich aristocrats. This type of funeral was called a *munus*, which referred to a duty to the dead fulfilled by their family. This posthumous obligation served two purposes—it honored the dead while raising the profile of the family hosting the event. The family name was all-important in ancient Rome, especially among the patricians, the ruling class, and the handful of aristocratic families that controlled the Senate. The achievements of the dead served not only as a reminder for the living, but also as a glittering signpost against which family members were encouraged to measure themselves. A *munus*, then, provided a perfect excuse to show off the position and status of the living under the guise of the accomplishments of the dead. For this reason, the privately funded *munus* became an increasingly lavish and expensive occasion designed specifically for the entertainment of a crowd.

The first recorded Roman *munus* took place in 264 BCE to honor an aristocrat called Junius Brutus Pera. At this *munus*, three pairs of gladiators—called *bustuarii*, after *bustum*, or funeral pyre—fought each in the city's Forum Boarium. Nearly 50 years later in 216 BCE, a three-day *munus* was held for Consul Marcus Aemilius Lepidus. Performing at this *munus* were 22 pairs of gladiators who fought in the larger Forum Romanum. Then, in 183 BCE, a much grander *munus* took place in honor of Publius Licinius. It lasted for three days, featured 60 pairs of gladiators and saw free handouts of meat for the spectators.

Above: Consul Marcus Aemilius Lepidus was a popular war hero, aristocrat and consul whose *munera* were held over a three-day period.

Facing page: A medieval interpretation of combatants at Roman *munera* from the Republican era.

In the years to come the *munus* grew in size and popularity. As Rome expanded its borders, its aristocrats grew wealthier and their *munera* became more extravagant.

The public attitude also changed, and it was expected that every *munus* would be a spectacular event followed by a banquet. The food supplied was impressively exotic fare, which included boar, wild fowl, and sow's udder. At this time, no cost was too great for high-profile aristocrats eager to curry favor with the people of Rome.

Portents and Omens

Roman historian Livy's account of the *Ludi Apollinares* is notable not only as an historical document but also as a record of the superstitious way the Romans viewed the world. Although portents and omens of doom were to be taken seriously, they could also be prevented if the right offering or sacrifice was made to the gods:

"The Games of Apollo had been exhibited the previous year, and when the question of their repetition the next year was moved by the praetor Calpurnius, the Senate passed a decree that they should be observed for all time. Some portents were observed this year and duly reported. The statue of victory which stood on the roof of the temple of Concord was struck by lightning and thrown down on to the statues of Victory which stood above the facade in front of the pediment, and here it was caught and prevented from falling lower. At Anagnia and Fregellae the walls and gates were reported to have been struck. In the forum of Subertum streams of blood had flowed for a whole day. At Eretium there was a shower of stones and at Reate a mule had produced offspring. These portents were expiated by sacrifices of full-grown victims; a day was appointed for special intercessions and the people were ordered to join in solemn rites for nine days."

—Livy, *The History of Early Rome*, translated by B.O. Foster

Livy's monumental *History of Rome* in 142 books became a popular classic during his own lifetime.

Right: The ruins of the *Forum Romanum* remain a popular destination for modern tourists.

LUDI

During the early Roman Republic, *munera* were privately funded and not regulated by the state. Instead the state provided its own public games called *ludi*, usually held to give thanks to the gods or commemorate a military victory. The oldest ludi were the *Equirria* and *Consualia*, horseracing spectacles that were dedicated to the gods Mars and Consus. As the Republic wore on, more *ludi* were added to the Roman calendar. The *Ludi Florales* were held during the spring to encourage a

> *"When everyone had had plenty to eat and drink they called for the gladiators. The moment anyone's throat was cut, they clapped their hands in pleasure."*
>
> —*Nikolaos of Damascus*

good harvest. Attendees wore multi-colored clothes and enjoyed various circus games that culminated in a sacrifice to the goddess Flora.

The *Ludi Apollinares* were instituted in 212 BCE during Rome's second Punic War against their bitter enemies, the Carthaginians. The aim of the *ludi* was to request the god Apollo's help in expelling the Carthaginians from the city of Capua, which had been seized by General Hannibal in 216 BCE. Famously, the first *Ludi Apollinares* was actually interrupted when a cry went up that the enemy was at the gates. Assuming Hannibal had finally arrived to sack Rome, the spectators duly ran for their weapons before finding it had been a false alarm. The cry *"Hannibal ante portas"*—"Hannibal before the gates!"—quickly became a popular proverbial phrase. In the end Hannibal was ousted from the Italian peninsula, and in 211 BCE Capua was recaptured by the Roman legions. The *Ludi Apollinares* continued to be celebrated annually from that point on.

The *Ludi Apollinares* provided spectators with the two most common forms of Roman entertainment outside of the *munera*: theater (*ludi scaenici*) and chariot racing (*ludi circenses*). Roman theater consisted of mime, comedy, and pantomime, which was mostly bawdy slapstick played for laughs. Many Roman patricians felt the theater was an affront to Roman values and made a point of vetoing the shows. This attitude was also upheld by the Senate, which decreed that no stone buildings could be constructed for

theatrical performances. Instead, wooden buildings had to be erected and then demolished again for every show. The Roman elite's abhorrence of everything theatrical continued throughout its history. Actors were considered *infamis*, the disgraced, and only slightly higher than gladiators in the social order. Emperor Nero's dalliances with the stage became the final insult that led his own Praetorian Guard to turn against him. Roman senator and writer Tacitus also mentions the theater with the same incredulity as he does gladiatorial games:

> "There are the peculiar and characteristic vices of this metropolis of ours, taken on, it seems to me, almost in the mother's womb—the passion for play actors and the mania for gladiatorial shows and horse-racing."

—Tacitus, *The Annals*, Translated by Alfred Church and William Brodribb

Chariot racing, by comparison to the theater, was a universally loved and passionately defended spectator sport in Rome. Its popularity was such that Etruscan King Tarquinius Priscus founded the Circus Maximus to house the races and christened it with spectacular *Ludi Romani* that ran for several days in a row. Originally built of wood, the Circus was a large U-shaped arena, with stepped-seating for around 150,000 spectators.

The racing itself involved four teams—the reds, blues, greens and whites—each of which inspired fanatical loyalty from Roman fans of all classes. Nero was an ardent supporter of the event and even raced a chariot himself on occasion. Charioteers

usually drove teams of two to four horses around the central *spina* barrier for seven laps to complete a race. Each race was a furious, high-octane event where charioteers tied themselves into the chariots by their reins and did their best to encourage accidents among their fellow racers. Fatalities—equine and human alike—were common.

Enter the Animals

The *ludi* at the Circus Maximus took a new twist with the introduction of wild animals in the second century BCE. Exhibitions of exotic animals from newly conquered lands were of great interest to the

Above: The slaughter of elephants first began in the Circus Maximus at the end of a parade.

Facing page: A bas-relief depicts early *venatores* battling with a lion, panther, and bear.

Facing page: A scene from the Roman sacking of Carthage in 146 BCE. Carved into the wood of the catapult are the words used by the orator Cato at the end of every speech: *"Delenda est Carthago!"*—*"Carthage must be destroyed!"*

> *"The pleasure of the holiday lacked something, unless savage beasts, too, had their share in tearing men's bodies to pieces."*
>
> —*Tertullian*

Roman public. The more unusual and terrifying creatures had particular allure, with popular favorites including elephants, lions, tigers, bears, wild goats, and camels. Circus organizers paid handsomely to have animals from northern Africa and the Near East lured into cages and transported to the capital. After weeks spent caged aboard wagons and ships the animals would arrive at their destination half crazed with fear, starvation, and exhaustion. It is little wonder that when exposed to the glare and hullaballoo of the Circus, some animals were known to snap and attack the audience.

The poet Claudian describes the appeal of foreign animals to Roman citizens:

> "… beasts that are the joy of the rich amphitheater and the glory of the woods. Whatsoever inspires fear with its teeth, wonder with its mane, awe with its horns and bristling coat—all the beauty, all the terror of the forest is taken."
>
> —Claudian, *On Stilicho's Consulship*

Before long, it was decided to present these "terrors of the forest" in the environs of their natural habitats, albeit artificially created. Parading exotic animals around an arena was one thing, but seeing them in action was another. Whole forest "sets" made of trees, bushes, and logs were built in the Circus to provide a stage for the *venationes*, or animal hunts. During these events, the animals would be released from their cages into the manmade forests and then hunted down by the *venatores* with spears, bows and arrows.

Ludi at the Circus became the perfect occasion for Rome to display its power and dominion over animals from its recently acquired territories. This had begun early on, as the Roman legions made their first forays into nearby lands. In 252 BCE, Consul Caecilius Metellus returned to Rome from Sicily with over 100 war elephants he had captured during his victory over the Carthaginians. Pliny the Elder, a writer and military commander, reported that once the elephants had been paraded at the Circus Maximus they were slaughtered because nobody knew what to do with them.

Metellus's victory led to the First Punic War with Carthage that ended in Rome's conquest of Sicily. In 146 BCE, during the Third Punic War, Rome crushed the Carthaginians and razed their capital city to the ground. Such was the ferocity of the Roman flames that scorch marks can still be seen on the stone remains of this once mighty city-state. But Rome did not stop at Carthage. In the same year, Roman legionaries brutally suppressed an uprising in Corinth and then sacked the Greek city.

The effect of the military operations against Carthage and Corinth sent a clear message that dissent towards Rome would not be tolerated. It also brought a huge infusion of wealth into Rome's coffers. Most importantly, 146 BCE marked the year that Rome gained complete control of the western Mediterranean. It had simply proved itself to be an irresistible force that not even the greatest ancient civilizations could defeat.

But Rome's ascent to world superpower also heralded the arrival of a new, unforeseen force that changed the course of its history. These were the military "hard men": insatiably ambitious

generals who tore up the constitutional rulebook and dominated the final years of the Republic. To win popular support and draw a veil over their misdeeds, these men would supply increasingly lavish and extravagant games. The only thing that lay between them and complete power was the Senate, which, by its very design, was meant to prevent the rise of a king of Rome.

THE DECLINE OF THE REPUBLIC

As the Roman legions steamrolled their way over foreign civilizations, the Senate at home behaved as if nothing had changed. But Rome's great acquisitions of conquered lands and the booty that came with it changed everything.

For centuries the Senate had been controlled by the equestrians, a handful of elite aristocratic families who monopolized all of the major offices of government. These families were becoming obscenely rich from the wagonloads of plundered wealth rolling in from abroad. Many spent large fortunes buying the smallholdings owned by peasant farmers in their creation of large, consolidated estates.

As the men from these smallholdings had been called up to serve in the army no one had been left to tend the fields, and often the farms were crippled by debt. Powerful senators armed with bulging bags of war profits then made short work of buying them off. The farmers had little choice but to join the increasingly large numbers of dispossessed Plebeians looking for work in Rome. It is no wonder that this group, which included unemployed army

veterans, became a disaffected mass that bubbled and seethed under the senatorial plutocrats.

The senators themselves chose to ignore the plight of the Plebeians, as one proverbial golden harvest after another filled their overstuffed granaries. It seemed there was little anyone could do to tip the balance until two idealistic senatorial brothers, Tiberius and Gaius Gracchus, stepped

Above: In 122 BCE, Gaius Gracchus met the same fate as his brother Tiberius. He was stabbed to death and his body thrown into the Tiber. Some 3,000 of his supporters were also killed.

Facing page: Here, Tiberius Gracchus removes Tribune Octavius from power through a vote in the popular assembly.

"Sulla … shouted orders to set fire to the houses, and seizing a blazing torch, led the way himself."

—*Plutarch*

into view. The Gracchi had one popular mandate: to pass land reforms that would restore some semblance of a fair and just republican system.

The Gracchi's reforms aimed to redistribute the new lands inherited by Rome, return farmland seized during the senatorial land grab, and create a grain ration for the Plebeians. As these measures were obviously unthinkable to the Senate, the Gracchi got themselves elected as Popular Tribunes to push them through. This was an office of government set up to protect the interests of the Plebeians, and had the power to pass legislation through the Popular Assembly. As the Gracchi delivered this fatally effective political maneuver, all the Senate could do was sit and rage.

The resulting retaliation took the familiar route of sudden personal violence. In 133 BCE, several senators clubbed Tiberius to death on Capitol Hill, and nine years later his brother Gaius was similarly dispatched. Interestingly, Gaius's murder took place in the same year that he removed the seating in a Roman arena to provide free standing room for the public.

This did nothing to endear Gaius to the magistrates who were set to pocket the profits from this rented seating. The rulers of Rome hated the Gracchi and in the end the corpses of both brothers ended up in the Tiber—the gravest of insults reserved only for the most disgraced and dishonorable enemies of Rome.

The senatorial murders of the Gracchi created a brutal and bloodthirsty precedent that also shone a light on the murky machinations of the Roman Republic. But the political damage had been done. The Gracchi had revealed a legal loophole that made it possible to bypass the stranglehold the Senate had on Rome.

Now, any ambitious young politician could simply become a Popular Tribune and make his way to the top by passing his personal legislation through the Popular Assembly. For the Senate, however, this new system would deliver an ugly and unforeseen twist of the knife. The men who followed the Gracchi's example were not cultivated young politicians with an idealistic hankering to change things for the better. Instead, they were powerful military leaders whose only aim was to advance themselves and seize power.

Rise of the Generals

The first of these military hard men was Lucius Cornelius Sulla, a gifted and controversial general with blotchy red skin and steel-gray eyes. At this time in Rome's history there was no provision for paying its soldiers. Instead each general was individually responsible for remunerating his legionaries from the plunders of war. As such, Rome's military leaders were fiercely supported by essentially private armies that answered to their general first and the state second.

Sulla's glittering military achievements had won him the consulship and the coveted *Corona Graminea* (grass crown). But when his commands were threatened by conniving senators, Sulla simply marched his army on Rome. Crossing the Rubicon—a shallow muddy-red river in northeast

CARBON
MARIUS
SIPION
NORBANUS
SERTORIUS
SORANUS
AQUILLIU
CECILIUS
ARELIUS
FAUSTUS
PERPERNA
DOMITIUS
STHENIUS
EM

Italy—was the most symbolically hostile action a general could take, and in doing so Sulla put the first of a series of nails into the Republic's coffin.

Following a second seizure of Rome in 82 BCE, Sulla began his proscriptions—lists of supposed enemies of the state that were posted in the Forum. A brutal reign of terror followed. Most of the proscribed simply went permanently missing, while the heads of others showed up on spikes in the Forum. Slaves freed by Sulla, each of whom was thereafter named Lucius Cornelius, carried out the killing. The numbers of the proscribed swelled as Sulla's cronies arbitrarily added new names to the list. The total murdered was said to have reached 9,000 by the end. With the money and assets seized from the proscribed, Sulla was able to pay the menacing 120,000-strong army that stood behind him. The rattled Senate could do little more than stand meekly by and reward Sulla for his tyranny with the position of dictator.

Oddly, in the end, with his complete control legitimized by the Senate, Sulla set about trying to restore its powers. He disabled the Popular Tribunate and Popular Assembly and made it impossible for generals to lead their armies into war without the Senate's agreement. Sulla then retired to his villa in 79 BCE to lead a life of debauchery. He died a year later, probably from liver failure.

Sulla's legacy was to provide his political heirs with the formula needed to kill off the Republic. These men—Gnaeus Pompeius Magnus and Gaius Julius Caesar—would ultimately go on to serve as the Republic's morticians.

Gnaeus Pompeius Magnus, or Pompey for short, was an aggressively ambitious aristocrat who rose to glory as one of Sulla's generals. His victories on the battlefields of Africa, Spain, and against the pirates of the Mediterranean won him popular support in Rome and the relevant offices, military commands, and triumphs from the Senate. Pompey was even spectacularly recalled from his campaigns to help suppress the gladiator rebellion led by Spartacus, a job all but done by the time of his arrival but one for which he took full credit.

After Sulla, the Senate was naturally wary of Pompey, especially after he was once ominously overheard to remark: "If Sulla could, why can't I?" To follow the path trod by his former leader, Pompey first set about reversing Sulla's final actions as dictator. He restored the powers of the Popular Tribune and Popular Assembly and quickly installed his own friends in these offices. In this way, Pompey was able to veto any senatorial legislation he considered unpalatable and instead pass his own through the Assembly. He then joined forces with Marcus Crassus and Julius Caesar to form the First Triumvirate, an alliance created to further each man's fortunes by undermining the Senate. In the end, war, greed, ambition, and betrayal left all three members of the Triumvirate heaped on the burial mound alongside the Roman Republic.

JULIUS CAESAR
Caesar was a brilliant general, orator and politician who knew the power of Rome lay in pleasing

Facing page: Sulla's proscriptions were lists of his enemies posted in the Forum. Each one of the proscribed was duly murdered and his estate seized to pay Sulla's soldiers.

"If Sulla could, why can't I?"

—Pompey the Great

Caesar's Spectacles

Suetonius was a first-century-CE aristocrat famous for his biographies of the Roman emperors. Here, he recounts the spectacles of Julius Caesar:

"His public shows were of great variety. They included a gladiatorial contest, stage-plays for every quarter of Rome performed in several languages, chariot races in the Circus, athletic competitions and a mock naval battle. At the gladiatorial contest in the Forum, a man named Furius Leptinus, of patrician family, fought Quintus Calpenus, a barrister and former senator, to the death. The sons of petty kings from Asia and Bithynia danced the Pyrrhic sword dance. One of the plays was written and acted by Decimus Laberius, a Roman knight, who forfeited his rank by so doing; but after the performance he was given five thousand gold pieces and had his gold ring, the badge of equestrian rank, restored to him—so that he could walk straight from stage to orchestra, where fourteen rows of seats were reserved for his Order. A broad ditch had been dug around the race-course, now extended at either end of the Circus, and the contestants were young noblemen who drove four-horse and two-horse chariots or rode pairs of horses, jumping from back to back.

The so-called Troy Game, a sham fight supposedly introduced by Aeneas, was performed by two troops of boys, one younger than the other. Wild-beast hunts took place five days running, and the entertainment ended with a battle between two armies, each consisting of 500 infantry, 20 elephants and 30 cavalry. To let the camps be pitched facing each other, Caesar removed the central barrier of the Circus, around which the chariots ran. Athletic contests were held in a temporary stadium on the Campus Martius, and lasted for three days.

The naval battle was fought on an artificial lake dug in the Lesser Codeta, between Tyrian and Egyptian ships, with two, three, or four banks of oars, and heavily manned. Such huge numbers of visitors flocked to these shows from all directions that many of them had to sleep in tents pitched along the streets or roads, or on roof tops; and often the pressure of the crowd crushed people to death. The victims included two senators."

—Suetonius, *The Twelve Caesars*,
translated by J.C. Rolfe

Left: Suetonius's *The Twelve Caesars* combined factual information with scandal and gossip, securing the author lasting fame.

its people. And nothing pleased the people more than a good show. Born in 100 BCE to an old Roman family, Caesar ruthlessly exploited *ludi* and *munera* to garner popular support and enable his meteoric rise through the public offices—Quaestor, Aedile, Pontifex Maximus.

Described by Suetonius as "tall, fair, well-built and something of a dandy, always keeping his head carefully trimmed and shaved," Caesar spared no expense in his public shows. Early on in his career, Caesar organized a *ludus* at the Circus Maximus that included the import of 400 lions for a *venatio*. To pay for these spectacles Caesar borrowed heavily against the promise of his future successes.

Self-promotion and publicity were key in Caesar's strategy, and it was for this reason that the

Above: This first-century-BCE tomb stone relief from Ephesus, Turkey, shows three gladiators engaged in combat. The gladiator to the far right armed with the trident is probably a *retiarus*.

munus he put on for his father was unlike any that had come before. It also occurred 20 years after his father had died, which led Tertullian to observe: "This class of public entertainment has passed from being a compliment to the dead to being a compliment to the living."

News of Caesar's forthcoming *munus* alarmed the Senate, which immediately limited the number of gladiators used at any *munera* to 320. The official justification was that assembling hundreds of armed gladiators in one place was a danger to the state—the recent revolt by Spartacus being a case in point. But in reality, Caesar himself was being restricted, the Senate nervous about what part an army of gladiators might play in fulfilling his obviously high ambitions.

In 59 BCE, Caesar, with the help of the First Triumvirate and a fortune in bribery money, was elected consul. This was followed by the military command of Gaul, where the spoils of war made Caesar rich. However, his burgeoning military and financial fortunes roused the envy of his Triumvirate partner Pompey, who was subsequently persuaded by senatorial whispers that there was room in Rome for only one great general. When the Senate decided to recall Caesar from his Gaulish command early, Pompey did not stand up for his supposed ally. With Crassus killed in battle, and Pompey and Caesar at loggerheads, the First Triumvirate had now completed its business.

The Senate presented Caesar with an impossible demand—return to Rome and give up your army. In doing so, Caesar would walk defenseless into

Right: According to Plutarch, Cicero said about Caesar: "When I look at his hair, which is arranged with so much nicety, and see him scratching his head with one finger, I cannot think that this man would ever conceive of so great a crime as the overthrow of the Roman constitution."

Left: In 49 BCE, Caesar led his army across the Rubicon River, the boundary between Italy and his province of Gaul.

Rewards and Reforms

In the end, Caesar crushed Pompey's armies and had his nemesis chased across Italy and Greece and into Egypt. He was said to have wept when Pompey's head was delivered to him. Now the undisputed master, Caesar was elected dictator for ten years by the Senate. This was the moment that Caesar could have ousted his enemies by replicating Sulla's reign of terror. But instead he was merciful and generous towards those who had wished him dead. This, in the end, was to prove a fatal error.

For a while, before his mortal undoing, Caesar proved he could be as charitable with the people of Rome as he had been with his murderous opponents in the Senate. He instituted grand building projects that provided work for the unemployed, he alleviated poverty through debt reform, and he provided the most lavish games yet seen in Rome. His land reforms were even based on those of the idealistic Gracchi. Caesar's gifts to the public are further described by Suetonius:

"He began building a new Forum with the spoils taken in Gaul, and paid more than a million gold pieces for the site alone. Then he announced a gladiatorial show and a public banquet in memory of his daughter Julia—an unprecedented event; and, to create as much excitement among the commons as possible, had the banquet catered for partly by his own household, partly by the market contractors.

whatever fate the Senate was planning for him. Instead, he followed the lead of Sulla and crossed the Rubicon with his army. Rome's bloodiest civil war ensued.

The Senate's part in the war, however, was as confused as its decision to pit Pompey against Caesar. In its struggle to preserve the virtues of the Republic and prevent tyranny, it was supporting one narcissistic general who would just as soon crown himself king as the general he was charged with defeating. The grand ideals of the Republic had now slipped from view as the military hard men seized control. The age of the Republic was turning into the age of the individual, and the new Roman Empire was one knife thrust away from being ruled by an emperor.

Above: After his victory over Pompey, Caesar was made dictator and awarded a triumph by the Senate. Triumphal games featuring *venationes* and gladiator contests followed.

He also issued an order that any well-known gladiator who failed to win the approval of the Circus should be forcibly rescued from execution and reserved for the coming show. New gladiators were also trained, not by the usual professionals in the schools, but in private houses by Roman knights and even senators who happened to be masters-at-arms. Letters of his survive, begging these trainers to give their pupils individual instruction in the art of fighting. He fixed the daily pay of the regular soldiers at double what it had been. Whenever the granaries were full he would make a lavish distribution to the army, without measuring the amount, and occasionally gave every man a Gallic slave."

—Suetonius, *The Twelve Caesars*, translated by Thomson and Forester

Alongside Caesar's games, the people of Rome were given presents: 10 bushels of grain, 10 pounds of oil, and 400 sestertii for each citizen. Caesar also handed out free meat and twice provided breakfast for the whole city. The age of "*panem et circenses*"—bread and circuses—had arrived. With it, the true nature of the *munera*, once a religious ceremony held to honor the dead, was made clear. Simply, Caesar had turned it into a king's gift to his

The Murder of Caesar

"As soon as Caesar took his seat, the conspirators crowded around him as if to pay their respects. Tillius Cimber, who had taken the lead, came up close pretending to ask a question. Caesar made a gesture of postponement, but Cimber caught hold of his shoulders. 'This is violence!' Caesar cried, and at that moment, as he turned away, one of the Casca brothers with a sweep of his dagger stabbed him just below the throat. Caesar grasped Casca's arm and ran it through with his stylus; he was leaping away when another dagger blow stopped him. Confronted by a ring of drawn daggers, he drew the top of his gown over his face, and at the same time ungirded the lower part, letting it fall to his feet so that he would die with both legs decently covered. Twenty-three dagger wounds went home as he stood there. Caesar did not utter a sound after Casca's blow had drawn a groan from him; though some say that when he saw Marcus Brutus about to deliver the second blow, he reproached him in Greek with 'You too, my child?'"

—Suetonius, *The Twelve Caesars*, translated by Robert Graves

Above: *The Death of Julius Caesar* by Jean-Léon Gérôme (1824–1904)

subjects—some cheap thrills to pacify the *Populus Romanus*. It was a clever turn. Caesar knew better than anybody that it was the people who had the final say in Rome—the people who were only ever one grievance away from becoming a rioting mob. It was with the support of his armies and the Roman public that Caesar had taken the top job, King of Rome in all but name.

The problem was that Caesar had overlooked a different mob secretly scheming under his own nose—the Senate. On the Ides of March 44 BCE a group of senators cut Caesar down in the Curia of Pompey, a meeting hall in the complex of Pompey's Theater.

Purges and Propaganda

The assassins justified Caesar's murder as the necessary removal of a tyrant who was about to crown himself king. Their error was in assuming that the people of Rome had reached the same conclusion. They had not. For the Plebeians, Caesar was a champion and benefactor, a conquering hero who had brought them wealth, glory, food and entertainment. Caesar had also introduced sensible reforms and stable rule, a much-needed relief from the political machinations of the increasingly ineffectual Senate. The *Populus Romanus* loved Caesar, and now he was gone they bayed for his killers' blood.

Caesar's assassins planned to throw the dictator's body into the Tiber and seize his property in the time-honored tradition. But fearing the vengeance of Caesar's right-hand man and Consul, Mark Antony, they instead retreated to their villas to await news. Meanwhile, the reading of Caesar's will

took place in Mark Antony's home. Here it was revealed that Caesar had nominated his nephew Gauis Octavius as his heir. The same Octavian, a pale, sickly-looking 18-year-old, would become Augustus, Rome's greatest ruler who led the empire into a new age of emperors.

Caesar's funeral was an impassioned day of mourning, where Caesar's bloodied toga was put on display alongside an ivory funeral couch on the Campus Martius. Mark Anthony further agitated the already inflamed crowd by reading out the oath made by every senator pledging to watch over Caesar's safety. It was a theatrical stroke that sealed the fate of Caesar's assassins. The Second Triumvirate that followed—an alliance made up of Antony, Octavian, and Marcus Lepidus—instigated

Above: The *Populus Romanus* **quickly turned into an angry mob and ousted Caesar's assassins from the city.**

Facing page: **By displaying Caesar's bloodied toga and reading out the senatorial oath to protect the dictator, Mark Antony whipped the mourning crowd into a frenzy.**

a purge that gave no quarter when hunting down Caesar's enemies. As Suetonius reports:

> "Very few, indeed, of the assassins outlived Caesar for more than three years, or died naturally. All were condemned, and all perished in different ways—some in shipwreck, some in battle, some using the very daggers with which they had treacherously murdered Caesar to take their own lives."
> —Suetonius, *The Twelve Caesars*, trans by J.C. Rolfe

After Caesar's murderers were defeated at the 42 BCE Battle of Philippi, the Second Triumvirate carved up Rome's empire between them. Predictably, this power-sharing arrangement did not last. Octavian sent Lepidus into exile on trumped-up charges of rebellion and then set up a propaganda campaign against Mark Antony. Mark Antony and his mistress Cleopatra, the last pharaoh of Egypt, were then utterly defeated by Octavian at the naval battle of Actium. Both committed suicide afterwards.

In the end Octavian, or Augustus as he became known, was simply the last man standing following Caesar's death. The Senate, which had sealed its fate by killing Caesar, would now limp along in the background for the rest of its days, an institution of power in name only. Luckily Caesar had left his heir, and all those who followed him, the blueprint for imperial rule. To control your people simply buy their affections with *panem et circenses*—bread and circuses. As the imperial age wore on, these games would reach a scale of extravagance unimaginable under the Republic. It was the rise of the emperor and the imperial cult that turned the games from simple duels at funeral ceremonies to vast spectacles of butchery and bloodshed. The days of the Republic—when restrictions were once put on the numbers allowed to die in the arena—were now well and truly over.

SPARTACUS

Most of our information about gladiators comes from funerary inscriptions, mosaics, and weaponry from archeological sites, such as the city of Pompeii. Occasionally a contemporary writer describes the feats of heroic gladiators, such as Martial's account of Priscus and Versus, who fought an epic battle during the opening day of the Colosseum. But most of the gladiators remain faceless and unremembered, and their stories forgotten.

However, there is one better-known gladiator whose story has survived. Spartacus was a former legionary who wanted nothing more than to escape the arena and return home. In doing so, he sparked a slave and gladiator revolution that nearly brought the Roman Republic to its knees.

Spartacus belonged to a *ludus*, or gladiator school, in Capua that had a particularly harsh reputation. Its gladiators were brutally treated, underfed and locked in chains when not in training. Spartacus had been sent to the *ludus* after deserting his legion and then being sold as a slave. His final sentence was to be the same as other proud and physically strong slaves—death or glory in the arena.

Facing page: The 31 BCE Battle of Actium ended in defeat for Mark Antony and Cleopatra and made Octavian the first emperor of Rome.

> *"Very few, indeed, of the assassins outlived Caesar for more than three years, or died naturally. All were condemned, and all perished in different ways."*
>
> —*Suetonius*

Right: The 1960 "sword and sandal" blockbuster *Spartacus* starred Kirk Douglas, cost an unprecedented $12 million, and featured an almost unknown director, Stanley Kubrick.

However, Spartacus did not sit and wait for his destiny. Instead, he and 78 other gladiators stole knives from the *ludus* kitchen, overpowered the guards and made their escape. The group, led by the Gauls Crixus and Oenomaus and the Thracian Spartacus, chanced upon a wagon carrying weapons to another *ludus*. Now armed, the gladiators made their way to the top of Mount Vesuvius where they set up a makeshift base.

> "He was a Thracian from the nomadic tribes and had great spirit and great physical strength."
>
> —*Plutarch*

When news of the gladiators' revolt reached Rome, the Senate dispatched Praetor Gaius Claudius Glaber to deal with the escapees. Although no one considered the gladiators a serious threat, Glaber marched at the head of 3,000 legionaries to make sure. He set up camp at the bottom of Mount Vesuvius, which effectively blocked off the gladiators' only exit as there was only one pathway

KIRK DOUGLAS   LAURENCE OLIVIER   JEAN SIMMONS   CHARLES LAUGHTON   PETER USTINOV   JOHN GAVIN   AND TONY CURTIS AS ANTONINUS

A STANLEY KUBRICK FILM

SPARTACUS

FILMED IN SUPER TECHNIRAMA 70

Left: A nineteenth-century magazine illustration shows Spartacus performing in the amphitheater in Capua.

up or down. A mini-siege then ensued, but Glaber had fatally underestimated the gladiators' cunning, as Plutarch describes:

> "The top of the hill, however, was covered with wild vines and from these they cut off all the branches that they needed, and then twisted them into strong ladders which were long enough to reach from the top, where they were fastened, right down the cliff face to the plain below. They all got down safely by means of these ladders except for one man who stayed at the top to deal with their arms, and he, once the rest had got down, began to drop the arms down to them, and, when he had finished his task, descended last and reached the plain in safety. The Romans knew nothing of all this, and so the gladiators were able to get round behind them and to throw them into confusion by the unexpectedness of the attack, first routing them and then capturing their camp."
> —Plutarch, *Life of Crasssus*, translated by Rex Warner

Gladiator Army

While Glaber fled, the gladiators killed his lieutenants and armed themselves with his soldiers' weapons. The news of Spartacus's victory spread rapidly, and before long tens of thousands of slaves had flocked to join him. Spartacus now rode at the head of a formidable gladiator army, one that wasted no time

in overrunning the various Roman camps and towns of Campania. The army's success was not surprising: it was no mere rabble of badly-equipped slaves, but a well-armed and experienced fighting force trained in the gladiator tradition by Spartacus and Crixus.

After a period of terrorizing the Italian mainland, the gladiator army began to be taken seriously by Rome. This time it sent out two legions under the command of Consuls Gnaeus Cornelius Lentulus Clodianus and Lucius Gellius Publicola. They were immediately successful. After a disagreement with Spartacus, Crixus had broken away from the main rebel force and taken with him the Gaulish and German gladiators. When Gellius caught up with Crixus he destroyed the breakaway group. Gellius's good fortune, however, was to be short-lived. His legionaries were defeated soon afterwards by Spartacus's army, which had already dispatched the legion under the hapless Lentulus.

Rome Prepares

The news alarmed the Senate. Not since the great Carthaginian general Hannibal marched his war elephants over the Alps had Rome been in danger of attack. However, it now appeared Spartacus had the numbers and military knowledge to be a serious

Strong, Great, and Terrible

Plutarch's account of Spartacus's campaign comes courtesy of his biography on Marcus Crassus. Plutarch describes Spartacus thus:

"He was a Thracian from the nomadic tribes and not only had a great spirit and great physical strength, but was, much more than one would expect from his condition, most intelligent and cultured, being more like a Greek than a Thracian. They say that when he was first taken to Rome to be sold, a snake was seen coiled round his head while he was asleep and his wife, who came from the same tribe and was a prophetess subject to possession by the frenzy of Dionysus, declared that this sign meant that he would have a great and terrible power which would end in misfortune. This woman shared in his escape and was then living with him."

—Plutarch, *Life of Crasssus*, translated by Bernadotte Perrin

Facing page: One of Spartacus's men comforts his leader as he dies. In reality, Spartacus was left to face his final destiny alone.

threat to the capital. The Senate turned in its hour of need to the celebrated general and aristocrat Marcus Licinius Crassus. Crassus had risen to prominence as one of Sulla's generals and was later the third member of the First Triumvirate, alongside Pompey and Caesar. He had become rich through Rome's overseas campaigns and the subsequent land grab in Italy, and later became the wealthiest man in Roman history. Crassus had raised an army at his own expense to deal with Spartacus, and now he set off in pursuit of the gladiator.

"He himself stood his ground, and, surrounded by the enemy, bravely defending himself, was cut in pieces."

—*Plutarch*

With Crassus at his heels, Spartacus retreated with his army through Lucania toward the southern coast of Italy. Here, he planned to make an escape to Sicily on Cilician pirate ships. In Sicily, Spartacus intended to form a great slave army capable of taking on Rome. But he was betrayed by the Cilicians and left stranded at the bottom of the Italian peninsula.

Fearing the rebels would turn and march on Rome, Crassus commanded his army to dig a ditch that would cut Spartacus off and stop him moving north. Crassus had had varying fortunes with his army and instituted the practice of decimation—the execution of one in every ten soldiers, drawn by lots—after several hundred of his men deserted. Plutarch explains:

"This was a traditional method of punishing soldiers, now revived by Crassus after having been out of use for many years. Those who are punished in this way not only lose their lives but are also disgraced, since the whole army are there as spectators, and the actual circumstances of the execution are very savage and repulsive."

—Plutarch, *Life of Crasssus*, translated by Rex Warner

Despite showing his men that they had more to fear from their general than Spartacus, Crassus must have felt the odds were stacked against him. Rattled, he sent word asking the Senate to call back Pompey from his campaign in Spain, and Lucullus from Thrace. It was a sensible precaution: Spartacus dealt with Crassus's ditch simply by filling in a section with fallen trees and leading his army across it. But the tide had turned for the gladiator-general. Overtaken by hubris, Spartacus's men demanded that they march to meet Crassus's army head on. Faced with a mutiny, Spartacus reluctantly assented to his men's request and readied his army for its final assault. The scene is described by Plutarch:

"Spartacus, seeing there was no avoiding it, set all his army in array, and when his horse was

brought him, he drew out his sword and killed him, saying, if he got the day, he should have a great many better horses of the enemies, and if he lost it, he should have no need of this. And so making directly towards Crassus himself, through the midst of arms and wounds, he missed him, but slew two centurions that fell upon him together. At last being deserted by those that were about him, he himself stood his ground, and, surrounded by the enemy, bravely defending himself, was cut in pieces."
—Plutarch, *Life of Crassus*, translated by Rex Warner

Unluckily for Crassus, Pompey arrived just in time to pick off many of the stragglers from Spartacus's army, and then took full credit for suppressing the rebellion. He was subsequently awarded a full triumph in Rome, whereas Crassus received only a simple ovation. Crassus, however, showed no mercy to the 6,000 prisoners of war captured from Spartacus's army. Every one of them was crucified along the Appian Way, the original Roman road built to suppress the uprising of the Samnite people in 312 BCE.

Spartacus was a lowly gladiator who had shaken the very foundations of Rome, but his legacy was a dazzling single event. Always true to its pragmatic nature, Rome learnt the lessons from the gladiator uprising and modified its systems to stop it ever happening again. In practice, this meant keeping gladiators locked up when they were not in training, and carefully stowing away their weapons at the end of each day. Rome would never again be threatened by a gladiator uprising.

The Emperors' Games

The gladiatorial games held under Augustus surpassed any that had come before. Vast sums were spent trying to devise new and ingenious ways of slaughtering men and animals for the entertainment of thousands of baying spectators. Now an emperor's gift to his people, Augustus's games set the standard for every ruler who followed.

By 27 BCE, Augustus had defeated his enemies and emerged as the triumphant survivor of Rome's bloody civil wars. He now made a great show of returning power to the Senate. The Senate, in turn, waited anxiously to see whether Augustus would crown himself emperor. Instead, Augustus simply sidestepped the issue, consolidating his position as undisputed leader of Rome under a new senatorial title: *Princeps*, or "First Citizen of Rome." He then took control of most of the empire's provinces, while leaving a minority under the Senate. Of course, the Senatorial provinces tended to be the ones without standing armies in case anyone harbored rebellious intentions.

Facing page: Gladiators fight before the emperor in this modern imagining of combat in the arena. In reality, an emperor would never have sat so close to the combatants.

Right: Gaius Octavius, or Augustus as he became known, was Rome's first emperor in all but name.

AUGUSTUS (63 BCE–14 CE)

Augustus encouraged the Senate to maintain a facade of power—it would meet, debate issues, and pass legislation on minor issues, such as building improvements. He even allowed the Senate to elect public officials, just as long as it picked from a list of candidates provided by Augustus. Sometimes the *Princeps* would keep up democratic appearances by attending the odd senatorial meeting himself. But in fact, Augustus ruled with absolute authority. He retained the Republic in name, while reigning over it as *Primus inter pares*—"First Among Equals." But the traditions of discussion, debate, and dissent had long since departed the Senate house; few dared disagree with Augustus. His powerbase was Rome's armies, and he used them against any who opposed him.

Gripped by Paranoia

Although politically Augustus had the Senate under his thumb, he feared meeting the same fate

Left: Augustus introduced more than 200 years of stable rule known as the *Pax Romana.*

as Caesar. During a visit by praetor Quintus Gallius, Augustus was seized with terror when Gallius clumsily clutched at a set of writing tablets under his robe. Assuming the praetor to be concealing a blade, Augustus ordered him to be tortured; later he tore Gallius's eyes out and sentenced him to death. On another occasion, Augustus held interviews with senators in a move to reduce their number. Ten bodyguards flanked the *Princeps* and the robes of each senator were searched before they approached him. Under his own toga he wore a sword and a steel corselet.

Augustus took on several of the offices formerly held by Roman magistrates, giving him access to resources he needed to secure the people's affections. There was no doubt that Augustus would follow Caesar's policy of *panem et circenses*—bread and circuses. First, he provided free or cheap grain to Roman citizens. In 2 BCE he increased the number of *plebs frumentaria* or "people of the grain" to 200,000—one fifth of Rome's population. He also handed out cash: 300 sestertii per citizen from Caesar's estate, and another 400 sestertii from the spoils of war in 29 BCE.

Now that their wallets and stomachs were full, the *Populus Romanus* demanded stronger fare from their circuses. Augustus did not disappoint. He built new amphitheaters and a complex of grand marbled halls called the *Saepta Julia* to hold the contests. Augustus also provided grand spectacles

that took place outside of the arena. This included a *naumachia*, a naval battle that took place in a large, purpose-built lake measuring 1,800 feet (550 meters) by 1,150 feet (360 m), with a new aqueduct built to supply it. Augustus used 30 ships, including full-sized triremes and biremes rowed by slaves, alongside smaller vessels. Over 3,000 men dressed as soldiers spent a day battling to the death.

The Imperial Games

While *munera* during the Republican age had been exploited by ambitious aristocrats for political

Above: An engraving of a *naumachia*, or naval battle, being staged in an amphitheater.

Above: Under Augustus a day at the gladiatorial games was given a schedule that began with the *venatio*, or animal hunt, in the morning.

Right: Fights with lions were a particular favorite with spectators, but many lions never made it to the arena, dying on the sea voyage from Africa.

else's games. From 22 BCE, privately sponsored games were allowed only twice a year, with a cap of 120 gladiators and a total cost of 25,000 denarii. Of course, there were no such restrictions on the emperor's games, which could sometimes include thousands of gladiators and cost up to 170,000 denarii. Augustus also made sure he introduced new spectacles that celebrated his victories and kept the imperial cult at the forefront of the public's mind.

Augustus's games were held during scheduled dates in December and in March, and each spectacle ran for around six days. A day at the games would follow a standard order of events, which set the benchmark for the next 400 years. The morning featured the *venatio* as well as fights between animals and gladiators known as the *bestiarii*. Then a period of time was set aside in the middle of the day for public executions. Many spectators took a break for lunch or a siesta during the executions, especially the equestrians who considered them unrefined. However, everyone made sure to be in attendance for the eagerly anticipated afternoon event—the gladiator fights.

gain, the gladiator games would now and forever afterwards be bound up with the imperial cult, the political propaganda machine that turned the emperor into a god to be worshipped throughout the empire. To make certain that no aspiring patrician could compete with his spectacles, Augustus put heavy restrictions on everybody

The Things Done by Augustus

Augustus wrote up his accomplishments for the world to see. The *Res Gestae Divi Augusti* ("The Things Done by the Divine Augustus") reads like an extended résumé and was inscribed on two bronze pillars outside his mausoleum. One column describes the spectacles he organized:

> "Three times in my own name I gave a show of gladiators, and five times in the name of my sons or grandsons; in these shows there fought about ten thousand men. Twice in my own name I furnished for the people an exhibition of athletes gathered from all parts of the world, and a third time in the name of my grandson. Four times I gave games in my own name; as representing other magistrates twenty-three times. For the college of quindecemvirs, as master of that college and with Marcus Agrippa as my colleague, I conducted the Secular Games in the consulship of Gaius Furnius and Marcus Silanus. In my thirteenth consulship I gave, for the first time, the games of Mars, which, since that time, the consuls by decree of the senate have given in successive years in conjunction with me. In my own name, or that of my sons or grandsons, on twenty-six occasions I gave to the people, in the circus, in the forum or in the amphitheater, hunts of African wild beasts, in which about three thousand five hundred beasts were slain."

—Augustus, *Res Gestae Divi Augusti*,
translated by Frederick W. Shipley

Above: Augustus's counsellor Maecenas, a great patron of the arts, presents members of the artistic community.

Divine Looks

Augustus had no trouble portraying himself as the leader of the imperial cult whose brilliance was supposed to shine like a beacon across all of Rome's conquered lands. Suetonius describes his appearance:

"Augustus's eyes were clear and bright, and he liked to believe that they shone with a sort of divine radiance: it gave him profound pleasure if anyone at whom he glanced keenly dropped his head as though dazzled by looking into the sun … Augustus was remarkably handsome and of very graceful gait even as an old man; but negligent of his personal appearance. He cared so little about his hair that, to save time, he would have two or three barbers working hurriedly on it together, and meanwhile read or write something … His teeth were small, few and decayed; his hair, yellowish and rather curly; his eyebrows met above the nose; he had ears of moderate size, a nose projecting a little at the top and then bending slightly inward, and a complexion intermediate between dark and fair. Julius Marathus, Augustus's freedman and recorder, makes his height 5 feet 7 inches (1.7 m); but this is an exaggeration, although, with body and limbs so beautifully proportioned, one did not realize how small a man he was, unless someone tall stood close to him."

—Suetonius, *Lives of the Twelve Caesars*, translated by Thomson and Forester

Above: An allegorical representation of Augustus as a god sitting above his victorious army.

The link between the games and the imperial cult was strengthened by the emperor's presence. Here, in the arena, a complicated political relationship was formed between the emperor and the crowd. During the Republican age, the state had been represented by the senators, especially those of the equestrian order, who were supposedly providing democratic rule. Now the days of SPQR (the *Senatus Populusque Romanus*, or "the Senate and the People of Rome") were over, the public's expectations focused on one man—the emperor.

The *Pax Romana*

Over time, Augustus proved to be a canny and charismatic ruler, whose reign led to more than 200 years of relative stability, the *Pax Romana* or "Roman Peace." On the other hand, as Suetonius points out, "many of Augustus's acts won him the hatred of the people." Now, at Augustus's games, the public had the perfect venue to vent their rage against the man at the top. After all, freedom of expression had always been considered a basic Roman right. There were, of course, limits. In imperial Rome with an all-powerful emperor at the helm it was sometimes unwise to protest too loudly, as Consul Gaius Asinius Pollio neatly put it: "I'm saying nothing. It's not easy to inscribe lines against a man who can proscribe."

Nevertheless, many spectators, feeling protected within the crowd, voiced their displeasure. Demands for cheaper bread or lower taxes would often pick up momentum and become a loud group chant that echoed around the arena. At

other times the chants would reflect the crowd's desire for a gladiator to live or die. These included shouts of "*mitte*" ("let him go") or "*iugula*!" ("kill him"). The crowd would also indicate whether they thought a fallen gladiator should be finished off or allowed to live by sticking out a hand and turning their thumbs. In the arena it was customary for a

Above: A gladiator seeks advice from the crowd and emperor on whether to finish his opponent off. Their gesture to him was known as the "turning of the thumb."

Tragic Spectacle

Tiberius's unwillingness to provide gladiatorial games left the way open for speculators outside of Rome to organize their own contests. Starved of their favorite entertainment, the people of Rome were willing to travel for a show. This led to a tragedy in 27 CE at Fidenae, a town 5.0 miles (8 kilometers) north of Rome. Tacitus describes the events:

> "One Atilius, of the freedman class, having undertaken to build an amphitheater at Fidena for the exhibition of a show of gladiators, failed to lay a solid foundation to frame the wooden superstructure with beams of sufficient strength; for he had neither an abundance of wealth, nor zeal for public popularity, but he had simply sought the work for sordid gain. Thither flocked all who loved such sights and who during the reign of Tiberius had been wholly debarred from such amusements; men and women of every age crowding to the place because it was near Rome. And so the calamity was all the more fatal. The building was densely crowded; then came a violent shock, as it fell inwards or spread outwards, precipitating and burying an immense multitude which was intently gazing on the show or standing round. Those who were crushed to death in the first moment of the accident had at least under such dreadful circumstances the advantage of escaping torture. More to be pitied were they

Above: Tiberius and his wife Julia, the daughter of Augustus. Their enforced union was not a happy one.

> who with limbs torn from them still retained life, while they recognized their wives and children by seeing them during the day and by hearing in the night their screams and groans … Fifty thousand persons were maimed or destroyed in this disaster. For the future it was provided by a decree of the Senate that no one was to exhibit a show of gladiators whose fortune fell short of four hundred thousand sesterces, and that no amphitheater was to be erected except on a foundation, the solidity of which had been examined. Atilius was banished."

—Tacitus, *The Annals*, translated by Alfred John Church and William Jackson Brodribb

defeated gladiator to hold up his index finger, if he could, to plead for mercy. His opponent would look questioningly to the emperor's box, awaiting his signal. The emperor often scanned the crowd before delivering his decision: a thumb up or a thumb down. Savvy emperors would always take their cue from the people and obey their wishes. However, not all of Rome's emperors were that smart; several were of dubious intelligence and others were in fact dangerously insane.

But whatever the emperor's mental state, the gladiatorial games were about theater and he was expected to play his role. The aim was to show the emperor's eager participation while also maintaining his regal dignity. Augustus played the part with poise and precision. However, many of the emperors that followed him failed to provide such a convincing performance.

TIBERIUS (42 BCE–37 CE)

While Augustus laid the foundations for future imperial rule, Tiberius Claudius Nero was first to give the title Roman emperor its lurid reputation for vanity, debauchery, megalomania, and madness. Unanimously disliked by the public, Tiberius was stern, dour, and spoke with a great deliberation that infuriated his father-in-law, Augustus.

The writer Tacitus filled up several volumes of his *Annals* on Tiberius, and summed him up thus:

> "Tiberius Nero was of mature years, and had established his fame in war, but he had the old

Right: A magazine illustration shows a principal referee (*summa rudis*) overseeing a gladiator bout. There were strict rules governing gladiator contests, but we know little about them.

Below: Tiberius was an unpopular emperor who alienated the Roman public through his dislike of the gladiatorial games.

arrogance inbred in the Claudian family, and many symptoms of a cruel temper, though they were repressed, now and then broke out. He had also from earliest infancy been reared in an imperial house; consulships and triumphs had been heaped on him in his younger days; even in the years which, on the pretext of seclusion he spent in exile at Rhodes, he had had no thoughts but of wrath, hypocrisy, and secret sensuality."

—Tacitus, *The Annals*, Translated by Alfred Church and William Brodribb

Tiberius's one saving grace was his skill as a general. He was responsible for conquering a large swathe of modern-day Switzerland and expanding Rome's borders along the River Danube. But his fortunes were to change after he returned to Rome in 13 BCE to become consul. In 11 BCE, Augustus ordered Tiberius to divorce his beloved wife Vipsania so he could marry his daughter Julia. In a sullen reaction to the union, Tiberius abandoned his duties in Rome and slunk off to self-exile at his villa in Rhodes. Unfortunately for Augustus, Tiberius was his only viable heir and in 2 CE he was coaxed back to Rome to be groomed for the emperorship.

Right: A favorite punishment of Tiberius was to have people tortured and then thrown off the cliffs in Capri.

Facing page: Tiberius is shown at his villa in Capri, a bucolic setting for violence and depravity.

Thus, in 14 CE following Augustus's death, Tiberius began his reluctant reign. From the outset, Tiberius seemed to make it his business to be disliked by everyone. He alienated the Senate (he described the senators as "men fit to be slaves") and then did the same with the Roman people.

Although he improved Rome's finances and the quality of life of its people, Tiberius made his disdain for their beloved games clear. Aside from personally boycotting most spectacles already on the civic calendar, Tiberius went one step further by reducing the budgets for all public entertainments in Rome. Crucially, he also restricted the number of gladiators allowed to be shown at any non-imperial games, but did not fill the void with new games of his own.

In Rome, Tiberius would rarely attend the few gladiatorial games that were still being produced. Under Augustus, the games had become an occasion for the people and public to establish a relationship—under Tiberius no such relationship was formed. To further increase the gap between himself and his people, Tiberius retired in 26 CE to rule from his estate in Capri. Here, he was able to indulge his darkest impulses while the bureaucrats in the capital managed the day-to-day running of the empire.

Sex and Sadism

Tiberius's appetite for sadism and sexual depravity was well documented by the contemporary historians of Rome. He delighted in torturing people and throwing them off the cliffs at Capri, where soldiers below clubbed them with oars to make sure they were dead. Tiberius would also invite dinner guests to drink large quantities of wine and then have their genitals tied to prevent them from relieving themselves.

Tiberius murdered members of his family. He took such a dislike to his grandsons Drusus and Nero that he brought trumped-up charges against them, forcing the Senate to declare them enemies of the state. It is thought that Nero committed suicide after an executioner visited carrying a senatorial warrant, a noose, and hooks to pull his body into the Tiber. Drusus was locked away and starved for such a long period that he tried eating his own mattress. The bodies of both grandsons were chopped into pieces so small that it was difficult to collect them all for burial.

Tiberius needed little justification for his executions. He once sentenced a man to death for treason after he had allegedly cut the head from a bust of Augustus and replaced it with another. He later confessed to the crime under torture. From that point on people could be executed for criticizing anything Augustus had done, or even for carrying a coin bearing his head into a lavatory or brothel.

Senators who offended Tiberius often slashed their own wrists, knowing a verdict of guilty would be passed against them in the courts. On hearing of one such act, Tiberius ordered his men to collect the accused, bandage up his wounds, and take him half-dead to prison.

Perhaps if Tiberius had not been so dismissive of his predecessor's prescription for bread and circuses his fate would have been different. The Roman people tolerated high levels of debauchery from the emperors who followed Tiberius, but they would not be denied their entertainment. One thing was certain—by the time of his death in 37 CE, Tiberius was hated by both Plebeians and patricians alike. The Senate refused to give Tiberius divine honors and the people shouted "To the Tiber with Tiberius"—the sharpest of Roman humiliations.

It is ironic, then, that under Tiberius the Roman Empire prospered. Its borders were vastly extended and Tiberius left the imperial coffers overflowing with plundered wealth. His successor spared no time in spending the loot, but no Roman emperor would ever again keep the Roman public from its gladiatorial games.

CALIGULA (12–41 CE)

There could be no greater contrast between the public's opinion of the late Tiberius and his grandson and successor Caligula. During Tiberius's funeral a dense crowd greeted the new emperor with affectionate names such as "star," "chicken," "baby," and "pet." Later, when he fell ill, people flocked to Caligula's palace to hold vigils. Some volunteered to die instead of him and others promised to become gladiators if he recovered.

Gaius Julius Caesar Augustus Germanicus had been given the nickname Caligula, or "Little Boot," when he wore oversized military boots while on campaign with his father Germanicus. According

Facing page: A cameo of Tiberius alongside Augustus, Julius Caesar, and Caligula, seated above peoples conquered by Rome.

Below: Caligula was initially popular with his people, but he soon revealed himself to be a merciless tyrant and sadist.

Left: Caligula sits before his subjects underneath statues of the gods Castor and Pollux.

Facing page: This stone relief from Turkey shows two gladiators in combat. The man on the left is probably a *retiarius*, since he is armed with a trident.

to Suetonius, Germanicus the elder had "won such intense popular devotion that he was in danger of being mobbed to death whenever he arrived at Rome or took his leave again." After the departure of the greatly unpopular Tiberius it was natural that the public's love for Germanicus spilled over onto his son.

Caligula strengthened his popularity through every available means. He ordered great building works, a magnificent funeral for Tiberius, and opulent new games in honor of his late mother. There was no question of Caligula's love of the games—he was a zealous believer in the importance of drama, theater, and gladiatorial spectacles. A self-proclaimed singer and dancer, Caligula had acted his way out of an early grave on Capri where he had spent six years living with his grandfather.

Tiberius, it seems, had summoned his grandson to undertake a twisted rite of passage into manhood. Once there, Tiberius's servants tried to trick him into complaining about his monstrous grandfather. But instead, Caligula took up the role of unflappable bystander. Despite Tiberius's abuses, Caligula's obsequiousness to his grandfather caused others to say, "There never was a better servant, nor a worse master."

Hypocritical Host

Although a great admirer and provider of gladiatorial games, Caligula was often critical when other people also enjoyed them. Suetonius describes one such occasion:

> "He constantly tongue-lashed the equestrian order as devotees of the stage and the arena. Angered at the rabble for applauding a faction which he opposed, he cried: 'I wish the Roman people had but a single neck,' and when the brigand Tetrinius was demanded, he said that those who asked for him were Tetriniuses also. Once a band of five *retiarii* dressed in tunics, matched against the same number of *secutores* yielded without a struggle; but when their death was ordered, one of them caught up his trident and slew all the victors. Caligula bewailed this in a public proclamation as a most cruel murder, and expressed his horror of those who had had the heart to witness it."

—Suetonius, *The Twelve Caesars*, translated by J.C. Rolfe

Facing page: A gladiator is paraded before Caligula in his imperial palace in the lead-up to a spectacle.

Shared Vices

Caligula's performance almost certainly saved him being executed by Tiberius, who had killed his other grandsons. But it was just an act. Underneath his impassive exterior, Tiberius shared much of his grandfather's sadism. He liked to watch tortures and executions, and he dressed up in a wig and robe for night-long debauches. Tiberius both encouraged and discouraged these inclinations. While he hoped theater and singing might curb Caligula's behavior he was also well aware of his grandson's vices. He once noted that Caligula "was destined to be the ruin of himself and all mankind" and that he, Tiberius, "was rearing a hydra for the people of Rome, and a Phaeton for all the world."

There was no sign of these horrors during the first part of Caligula's reign. Instead he did all he could to please the people with the bread and circuses of Augustus. No expense was spared with lavish theatrical shows, vast handouts of food, gifts, and huge gladiatorial contests. Many of these were spiced with prizefights and boxing matches, and he also introduced new events such as panther baiting.

Caligula also produced a spectacle that recreated the building of Xerxes's bridge across the Hellespont. The Persian emperor had famously constructed the pontoon bridge in 480 BCE to invade Greece. To achieve his much larger bridge, Caligula anchored a line of ships across the Bay of Naples and covered them with planks and earth to create a Roman road. He then spent two days riding chariots up and down the road, pausing only to change horses and costumes.

Caligula also provided several games in the Roman provinces abroad, in particular an Athenian games at Syracuse in Sicily, and a gladiatorial spectacle at Lugdunum, Gaul. This included a competition in Greek and Latin oratory, where the losers were forced to erase their written entries with their tongues or risk being thrashed and flung into a nearby river.

The Tide Turns

After a year of Caligula's seemingly golden rule, trouble began. This was how long it had taken the emperor to spend the 2.7 billion sestertii left in Rome's coffers by Tiberius. Caligula had bankrupted Rome. He then became the kind of tyrant that Rome's former Republican senators would have glimpsed only in their most tortured nightmares.

Caligula's first act was to make the Roman people refill the empire's empty purse. He levied taxes on anything he could think of, including food, marriage, and prostitution. Then he seized the estates of rich equestrians, created a brothel in his palace made up of patricians' wives and children, and auctioned off the lives of gladiators at the games.

Caligula's behavior at home became increasingly bizarre. He had an incestuous relationship with his sisters and kept his sister Drusilla openly by his side in the manner of a wife, even though she was married to Consul Cassius Longinus. When Drusilla died, Caligula ordered a period of public mourning, making it a capital offense to laugh, bathe, or eat with family members. Caligula was not as fond of his other sisters, as according to writer Suetonius

Below: Julia Drusilla was the daughter of Caligula's mistress Caesonia, whom he claimed as his own. The emperor admired and encouraged the child's sadistic urges.

he "frequently prostituted them to his catamites" (a catamite being a young man involved in a sexual relationship with an older man). He was also in the habit of inviting for dinner patricians and their wives, who he would "examine very closely, like those who traffic in slaves." He would then leave the room, send for the woman he found most desirable, and later return to give the diners a graphic account of what had occurred.

Acts of Unspeakable Cruelty

Members of the Senate were often ordered to run for miles alongside Caligula's chariot, or stand dressed in short tunics by his dining couch, waiting for instructions. He ordered one out-of-favor senator to be torn limb from limb when he entered the Senate house and was not satisfied until his body parts were heaped at his feet. Senators were also ordered to attend the arbitrary execution of their sons, and when one excused himself because of ill-health, Caligula sent a litter to collect him.

Caligula's constant female companion was Caesonia, described by Suetonius as "neither handsome nor young, and … the mother of three daughters by another man." He often exhibited Caesonia to his soldiers, either naked or sometimes dressed up in military uniform. When she gave birth to a daughter, Caligula declared it to be his and named her Julia Drusilla—a child he apparently respected for her tendency to scratch at the eyes of other children.

Caligula's madness was both random and pointed. Gangly, pallid, and balding, he made it a capital crime for any person to look down at his thinning pate from above. He also resented any man with a full head of hair, and frequently ordered such men to shave their hair into ridiculous styles. Not all hirsute men got off so lightly, as Suetonius writes:

"There was one Esius Proculus, the son of a centurion of the first rank, who, for his great stature and fine proportions, was called the Colossal. Him he ordered to be dragged from his seat in the arena, and matched with a gladiator in light armor, and afterwards with another completely armed; and upon his worsting them both, commanded him forthwith to be bound, to be led clothed in rags up and down the streets of the city, and, after being exhibited in that plight to the women, to be then butchered."

—Suetonius, *The Twelve Caesars*, translated by Thomson and Forester

---

"I wish the Roman people had but a single neck."

—*Caligula*

It was at his spectacles that Caligula's insanity was left bare for everyone to see. On one occasion, an equestrian Caligula had condemned to be thrown to the lions began screaming his innocence. Caligula calmly had him dragged from the arena to have his

tongue ripped out before bringing him back in to continue the sentence. At another games, Caligula ordered the manager of the *venationes* be flogged for several days running, and only allowed him to be put out of his misery when "the smell of suppurating brains became unsupportable." Everyone was fair game at these events, as Suetonius describes:

"In the spectacles of gladiators, sometimes, when the sun was violently hot, he would order the curtains which covered the amphitheater to be drawn aside and forbad any person to be let out; withdrawing at the same time the usual apparatus for the entertainment, and presenting wild beasts almost pined to

Above: The Praetorian Guard assassinated Caligula after he had threatened to make his favorite horse, Incitatus, consul.

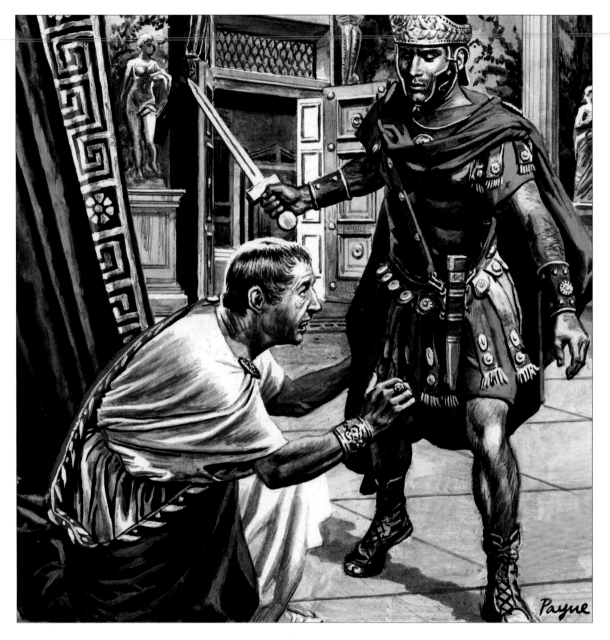

Left: After the assassination of his uncle Caligula, Claudius was found hiding behind a curtain. He reportedly fell to his knees and begged for his life.

death, the most sorry gladiators, decrepit with age, and fit only to work the machinery, and decent house-keepers, who were remarkable for some bodily infirmity."
—Suetonius, *The Twelve Caesars*, translated by J.C. Rolfe

But there was a limit, even for Caligula, who had begun appearing in the arena as a *thraex* gladiator. His fate was sealed when he made it known that he planned to make his favorite horse, Incitatus, consul. Incitatus already had its own marbled stable, a jewelled collar, purple blankets, and a house where it entertained human guests of Caligula's choosing. Although several conspiracies sprang up against Caligula at this time, it was his own Praetorian Guard that assassinated him—another Caesar stabbed to death by those charged with his protection.

CLAUDIUS (10–54 CE)

It was the commotion following Caligula's murder that caused Claudius, the emperor's uncle, to hide in fear behind a curtain in the royal palace. After dispatching Caligula, Caesonia, and their daughter Julia, the Praetorian Guard seized control of the city. Discovered by a legionary, Claudius dropped to the floor and clasped his knees, begging to be spared. The bewildered soldier ordered Claudius to be taken

Right: The Praetorian Guard was the emperor's elite bodyguard that became the power behind the throne: they deposed emperors and also crowned them.

in a litter to the Praetorian camp. The next day the Praetorian Guard took it upon itself to proclaim Tiberius Claudius Caesar Augustus Germanicus emperor.

While this was taking place, a long debate in the Senate house about who should become the new emperor showed just how irrelevant the institution had become. While some muttered about restoring the Republic, the senators backing this motion were notably in the minority. After several decades of emperors, the Senate and the people of Rome were prepared to maintain the imperial system. However, by the time the Senate had agreed that it did indeed want a new emperor, one had already been installed by Rome's new, ambitious powerbase—the Praetorian Guard.

During the Republic, the Praetorian Guard was an elite unit of soldiers charged with protecting their praetor or general in the field. Under Augustus, the guard was stationed in Rome to protect the emperor and included nine cohorts of 500 to 1,000 men. At any one time the Praetorian Guard, stationed in its camp just outside the city walls, would be a heavily armed 4,500-strong force ready for action.

After dislodging Caligula and enthroning Claudius, the guard proved itself to be highly corruptible. For the right price or simply of its own volition, the guard would assassinate and install

Expressions of Death

Although Claudius had won the public's admiration through his participation at his games, his appetite for brutality outside of the arena was little different from that of his imperial predecessors. Suetonius explains:

"That he was of a cruel and bloodthirsty disposition was shown in matters great and small. He always exacted examination by torture and the punishment of parricides at once and in his presence. When he was at Tibur and wished to see an execution in the ancient fashion, no executioner could be found after the criminals were bound to the stake. Whereupon he sent to fetch one from the city and continued to wait for him until nightfall. At any gladiatorial show, either his own or another's, he gave orders that even those who fell accidentally should be slain, in particular the net-fighters, so that he could watch their faces as they died. When a pair of gladiators had fallen by mutually inflicted wounds, he at once had some little knives made from both their swords for his use. He took such pleasure in the combats with wild beasts and of those who fought at noonday, that he would go down to the arena at daybreak and after dismissing the people for luncheon at midday, he would keep his seat and in addition to the appointed combatants, he would for trivial and hasty reasons match others, even of the carpenters, the assistants, and men of that class, if any automatic device, or pageant, or anything else of the kind, had not worked well. He even forced one of his pages to enter the arena just as he was, in his toga."

—Suetonius, *The Twelve Caesars*, translated by J.C. Rolfe

emperors and bully the Senate and people to do its bidding. Claudius, only too aware whose palms he needed to grease, awarded every member of the Praetorian Guard with a 15,000 sestertii "golden handshake" as his first imperial action.

Public Adoration

The Senate had hoped not to suffer another in the line of Julio-Claudian emperors, but the public loved Claudius. The new emperor understood the importance of bread, circuses and free grain and corn. He revived the older spectacles favored by Augustus as well as entirely new games "which no one had ever seen or would ever see again," according to Claudius himself. These included

Right: Tiberius was happy to provide the Roman public with new and novel games, but his degeneracy was little different from his imperial predecessors'.

Facing page: Claudius introduced new *venationes* that included wild animals fighting with the Praetorian Guard.

venationes held in the Circus, where panthers and bulls were hunted down by the Praetorian Guard, and gladiatorial contests that ran for several days at a time. Claudius also staged a mock-sacking of a British town on the Campus Martius that culminated in the surrender of the British "kings."

Claudius was also an active participant in the games and did not see the need to hide his enthusiasm behind a veneer of imperial dignity. He would address the audience as his "masters" and attempt to entertain them with jokes. He even used his left hand—considered a vulgar gesture for an emperor—to count out the gold coins paid to victorious charioteers and gladiators. He also once awarded the wooden sword of freedom to an *essedarius*, a type of gladiator who fought from a chariot, after the audience pleaded with him to do so. This merciful gesture met with such great applause that Claudius made it known that the people should all bear children, as they offered protection even to a gladiator.

On another occasion, Claudius held a *naumachia* on Lake Fucino, which, according to Tacitus, included 19,000 condemned criminals aboard large seafaring galleys. Around the edge of the lake, Claudius placed the Praetorian Guard armed with catapults and ballistas so that none of the fighters could escape. Thousands of spectators from Rome and its neighboring towns flocked to the *naumachia*, eager both to see the action and also to show their respect for the emperor.

But before the spectacle began, Claudius suffered an embarrassment. To signal the start of battle, the fighters greeted Claudius with the words "Hail Caesar, we who are about to die salute you." Contrary to popular opinion this is the only time in recorded Roman history that this phrase was used. In response, Claudius called back, "Or not, as the case may be," which the combatants took to mean

> ## *"That he was of a cruel and bloodthirsty disposition was shown in matters great and small."*
>
> —*Suetonius*

that they had all been pardoned and then refused to fight. At this Claudius flew into a rage and ran down to the lake's edge where Suetonius records that he "threatened and coaxed the gladiators into battle." The 24 trireme ships then began the combat.

While Claudius played a clever political hand by producing high numbers of spectacles, he appeared dimwitted in his personal life. Married four times, his wife Valeria Messalina was infamous throughout Rome for her infidelities. Claudius, however, was oblivious to them. But he did not fail to notice a plot against his life by Messalina and Consul Gaius Silius in 48 CE: both parties were executed, two of the many that Claudius had murdered for various offenses against him.

After Messalina, Claudius married his niece Agrippina and then passed a law making unions between uncles and nieces legal. Agrippina dominated Claudius and quickly became co-ruler of Rome in all but name. It was her ambition for her son Nero to become the next emperor in place of Claudius's heir by blood, Britannicus. After Claudius

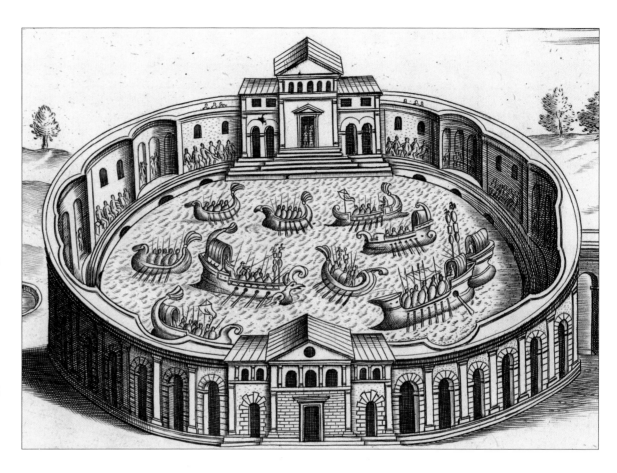

had made Nero his co-heir, Agrippina murdered him with a meal of poisonous mushrooms.

NERO (37–68 CE)
Nero Claudius Caesar Augustus Germanicus was only 17 when he was declared emperor by his mother Agrippina and the Praetorian Guard. He immediately made clear his intention to rule in the style of Augustus as a just and generous emperor

Above: Claudius's *naumachia* was reported to include 19,000 condemned criminals aboard large galleys.

Facing page: Claudius and his niece Agrippina, who the emperor married. He then passed a law allowing all other uncles to do the same.

and provide Rome with a long-lasting cultural legacy. For the first five years, Nero kept his word. He reduced taxes, banned capital punishment, and presented an immense variety of spectacles that included chariot races, parties and a gladiatorial contest with a twist. This took place in a wooden amphitheater near the Campus Martius, and featured a battle between hundreds of members from the equestrian class, including senators. These combatants were also required to fight wild beasts and to perform other duties around the arena. However, during the games Nero ordered that none should be slain, not even convicted criminals.

In place of the normal gladiatorial violence, Nero organized poetry competitions, stage plays, and athletic events. He even actively participated himself as a singer, musician, and charioteer. At a Great Festival held for the "eternity of the empire," Nero honored the other half of the bread and circuses tradition by giving out vouchers for grain, jewels, slaves, animals, apartments, ships, and farms.

Nero's theatrical ambitions were such that he often sang or read poetry on stage. He also bribed or bullied singers appearing alongside him to underperform. Nero made it illegal for anyone to leave the theater during his performances, including women who had gone into labor or men shamming death so they could be removed from their seats. Nero also raced chariots at the Circus Maximus, although the odds of victory were weighted heavily in his favor. At one show, Nero tried in vain to race a team of 10 horses, an ambitious feat that saw him fall face first into the Circus dirt. Although he was helped back into his chariot, Nero still failed to reach the finish line; luckily the officials deemed that he was the winner anyway.

Attempted Matricide

But Nero, like Caligula, was a psychological time bomb waiting to go off. He owed his power to his mother Agrippina, and she continued to dominate his rule. This was a toxic and violent relationship, truly a mixture of love and hate. The pair were said to have an incestuous union that showed itself whenever they traveled together in a litter. But Nero's hatred for Agrippina was equally fervent. Eventually he banished her from his palace, stood down her bodyguard and tried to poison her. After three attempts—each time Agrippina saved herself with an antidote—Nero arranged for the tiles above her bed to drop on her while she slept. But Agrippina learned of the plot and once again escaped unharmed.

Next, in a show of filial reconciliation, Nero invited Agrippina to dinner at his villa at the seaside resort of Baiae. After making sure the galley that had delivered her suffered an accidental collision, Nero offered Agrippina his private boat to take her home. The boat had been rigged to collapse once in deep water, and Nero sat up all night anxiously awaiting news. But he was foiled once again, learning the next morning that his mother's boat had sunk but she had managed to swim to shore. Nero's final attempt did not fail. In 59 CE he had Agrippina stabbed to death and the murder made to look like suicide.

Facing page: Nero sometimes starred in the Circus Maximus as a charioteer and once unsuccessfully tried to race a team of 10 horses.

"Above all Nero was carried away by a craze for popularity and he was jealous of all who in any way stirred the feeling of the mob."

—*Suetonius*

Nero then ordered the execution of his wife Octavia in 62 CE. The emperor was perhaps expecting trouble as a result, but nothing happened. Seemingly able to live a consequence-free life, Nero appeared to spin entirely out of control. He spent the last six years of his reign sinking deeper into degeneracy and madness.

Marriage and Murder

Nero often spent the evenings walking the streets of Rome looking for sexual encounters with men and women alike. He would also encourage his entourage of gladiators to start fights. He created a lakeside festival where guests on rafts floated towards each other, arranged by "age and experience in vice." On the shore brothels filled with noble women and prostitutes were lit up at night by torches and accompanied by bands of musicians. At one such event Nero married a Greek man call Pythagoras, taking on the role of the bride, as Tacitus describes:

> "The bridal veil was put over the emperor; people saw the witnesses of the ceremony, the wedding dower, the couch and the nuptial torches; everything in a word was plainly visible, which, even when a woman weds darkness hides."

—Tacitus, *The Annals*, Translated by Alfred Church and William Brodribb

According to Suetonius, in another marriage to a man called Doryphorus, in the honeymoon chamber Nero "went so far as to imitate the cries and lamentations of a maiden being deflowered."

Nero's actions divided Rome—he had executed many senators and made it clear he did not intend to spare the rest. Some of the senators had conspired against Nero, but, as he also executed any person on any pretext, the remainder of the Senate and all of the Roman aristocracy were understandably anxious about its survival. The masses, on the other hand,

Above: Nero and Agrippina turn their thumbs at a gladiator fight during a rare moment of family harmony.

Facing page: Nero tried several times to have his mother Agrippina murdered, but she survived every attempt. Finally she was stabbed to death and the assassination made to look like suicide.

> *"No sooner was twilight over than Nero would range about the streets playing pranks … he used to beat men as they came home from dinner, stabbing any who resisted him and throwing them into the sewers."*
>
> —*Suetonius*

held a different view, as Tacitus explains: "These and the like sentiments suited the people, who craved amusement, and feared, always their chief anxiety, scarcity of corn, should he be absent."

Nero made sure the Roman public was supplied with a generous supply of grain and put vast and violent gladiatorial games back into the civic calendar. The price of these spectacles was high, but money meant little to Nero. Luckily for the emperor, the empire continued to operate efficiently in the hands of its 10,000 bureaucrats. Rome worked while Nero played his hideous games.

To create spectacles never seen before, Nero built a new amphitheater and introduced gladiatorial fights between women. He also invented a new way of taking part himself, as Suetonius reports:

> "He so prostituted his own chastity that after defiling almost every part of his body, he at last devised a kind of game, in which, covered with the skin of some wild animal, he was let loose from a cage and attacked the private parts of men and women who were bound to stakes."

—Suetonius, *Lives of the Twelve Caesars*, translated by J.C. Rolfe

Fire and Fiddling

But Nero's glory days did not last. In 64 CE, a fire started in the Circus Maximus burned for nine days and destroyed most of the city. According to legend, Nero started the fire himself and played his fiddle while Rome burned. But in fact he was at his villa at Antium, 21.7 miles (35 km) away. Nevertheless, fingers were pointed Nero's way,

especially in light of his much-discussed plans for a reconstruction of Rome. Nero's Golden House—a planned 300-acre (121-hectare) luxury complex of palace buildings and grounds, expected to cover a third of the city when finished—was taken as further evidence of the emperor's guilt. Nero tried to deflect the accusations by blaming the Christians, whom he condemned as criminals, and persecuted in a brutal reign of terror that earned him the nickname "Antichrist."

Nero's megalomania had to end somewhere. As his extravagances had nearly bankrupted Rome, a predictable and unsupportable rise in taxes followed. But it was not his punishment of the Roman public for his overspending, nor his sexual perversions, nor even his many arbitrary executions that sank Nero. Instead it was his fondness for theater that ended his rule. When Nero appeared on the stage to play the parts of pregnant women and gladiators about to be executed, the Praetorian Guard decided that enough was enough. The guard joined forces with a rebellious army being led by the general Galba, and the Senate declared Nero to be an enemy of the state.

The Senate also issued an edict that Nero should die a slave's death on a cross and under the whip. Nero fled Rome and committed suicide in a villa outside the city. But while the senators and soldiers of Rome rejoiced at the news, Tacitus reported that the people did not:

> "The degraded populace, frequenters of the arena and the theater, the most worthless of the slaves and those who having wasted their property

Christian Executions

Nero's persecution of the Christians is often associated with the rise of martyrdom and is taken as proof of the immorality of the imperial cult of Rome. In the end, the Christian sect, still relatively small at the time of Nero, would far outlive the mighty Roman civilization. Here, Suetonius describes Nero's destruction of the Christians he blamed for the burning of Rome:

"Accordingly, an arrest was first made of all who pleaded guilty; then, upon their information, an immense multitude was convicted, not so much of the crime of firing the city, as of hatred against mankind. Mockery of every sort was added to their deaths. Covered with the skins of beasts, they were torn by dogs and perished, or were nailed to crosses, or were doomed to the flames and burnt, to serve as a nightly illumination, when daylight had expired. Nero offered his gardens for the spectacle, and was exhibiting a show in the circus, while he mingled with the people in the dress of a charioteer or stood aloft on a car. Hence, even for criminals who deserved extreme and exemplary punishment, there arose a feeling of compassion; for it was not as it seemed for the public good, but to glut one man's cruelty, that they were being destroyed."

—Suetonius, *The Twelve Caesars*, translated by Thomson and Forester

Above: Nero was a great persecutor of Christians: he would have them sewn into the skins of animals and savaged to death by wild dogs.

were supported by the infamous excesses of Nero, caught eagerly in their dejection at every rumor."

—Tacitus, *The Annals*, Translated by Alfred Church and William Brodribb

In Rome, it seemed, popular entertainment trumped every form of imperial vice and corruption.

The Julio-Claudian Dynasty Ends

Nero was last in the line of the Julio-Claudian emperors that had began with Augustus. But there was no question of a return to a Republic. Many senators had been executed or sent into exile. The survivors had either surrendered to Nero's tyranny or tried to ingratiate themselves to him; in neither case did they emerge with any credit. Instead the emperorship would fall to those who commanded the greatest armies in the imperial provinces.

The unstable nature of this arrangement saw three successive emperors—Galba, Otho, and Vitellius—rise and fall in a matter of months. The man who ultimately prevailed was Vespasian, a general and former consul who had the backing of the Roman legions of Egypt, Judaea, Syria, and the Danube. His armies marched on Rome and the Senate cravenly proclaimed Vespasian emperor. The new line of Flavian emperors had begun.

Vespasian had few close ties with the Senate, but made it his business to restore stability to Rome after Nero. This above all meant refilling Rome's coffers, which needed 40 million sestertii to strengthen the city's shattered infrastructure.

Facing page: An artist's impression of Nero taking his own life in 68 CE.

Below: A bronze *thraex* helmet discovered in the city of Pompeii.

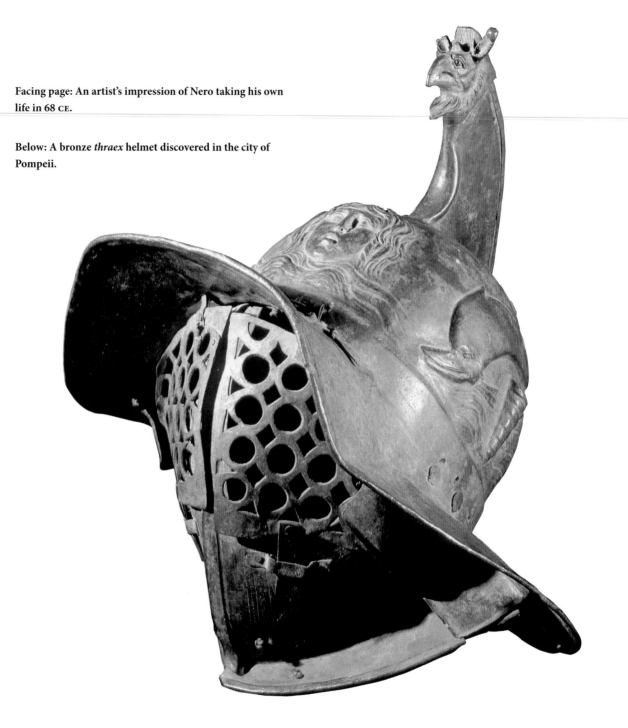

> *"At the dedication of his amphitheater he [Titus] gave a most magnificent and costly gladiatorial show … a combat of gladiators, exhibiting five thousand wild beasts of every kind in a single day."*
>
> —Suetonius

Rome was in ruins. Those parts not destroyed by fire were in the process of being demolished to make way for Nero's Golden House. Vespasian gave much of the land earmarked for this grand plan back to the people and put up great public buildings on the rest. The largest of these was a massive stone amphitheater that became known as the Colosseum.

The building of this immense charnel house won the hearts and minds of the people of Rome. Nero's wooden amphitheater had burned down, destroyed along with the tyrant emperor. In its place, the Colosseum was intended to eradicate the horrors of Nero from the public consciousness. It was a grand, generous, and healing gesture that celebrated the majesty of Rome while providing its people with their favorite entertainment—violence and slaughter.

When the Colosseum was finally completed in 80 CE under the emperorship of Vespasian's son Titus, it marked a new era for the gladiatorial games. This state-of-the-art amphitheater of death could house over 50,000 spectators and allowed killing on an unprecedented scale. Games sometimes ran for weeks at a time. The age of the gladiator contests as we now think of them had arrived.

The Gladiators

Gladiators were typically prisoners of war, condemned criminals, and slaves who had rebelled against the might of Rome. Once sentenced to a gladiator school, these men were stripped of all civil liberties and became *infamis*—the disgraced. However, sometimes senators, citizens, and other free men also became gladiators.

Prisoners of war made up most of the gladiator numbers during the heady days of the late Republic and early empire. As the Roman war machine steamrolled over one Mediterranean civilization after another, thousands of those who opposed it were clapped in chains and shipped back to Rome. Many of these once proud warriors then met their fate at spectacles such as the extravagant *naumachiae* held by Augustus and Claudius.

However, the nature of the gladiators changed as the empire aged. In 117 CE, Rome reached its zenith. This was the year that Emperor Trajan led his legions into the disputed territory of Parthia, in present-day Iran, and decided to press on into

Facing page: The turning of the thumb, *pollice verso*, indicated whether a defeated gladiator was allowed to live or die.

Right: A first-century-CE gladiatorial relief from Preturo, L'Aquila province, Italy.

Mesopotamia—the first Mediterranean ruler to do so since Alexander the Great. But the sight of this vast new country disconcerted the emperor. Gazing over the large swath of arid land before him, Trajan realized it was all too big and far away from Rome: the empire had gone as far as it could go.

From that point on, Rome stopped extending its borders and instead concentrated on controlling the territories within its empire. Rome believed it was generous in allowing those conquered people the chance to enjoy the benefits of Rome. As long as each territory paid its taxes and kept the *pax Romana*, it was free to bathe in the success that was the Roman Empire.

Above: *Ad flammas*, or death by flames, was a common sentence for criminals executed in amphitheaters. Nero went one step further by illuminating his games with Christians as flaming torches.

Facing page: A relief from the Sabratha Theater in Libya depicts a master rebuking his slave.

While Rome showed leniency towards those that accepted its rule, any who opposed it faced execution, enslavement, or a place at a *ludus*, the gladiator school. For Romans, this was the natural order. People who rebelled against Rome forfeited their right to a place in its society and deserved to die. Such rebels often met their fate in the arena by *ad bestias*, death by wild beasts, *ad flammas*, death by flames, or *ad gladium*, death by the sword.

After Rome stopped expanding, it recruited gladiators from among the rebels within its borders rather than, as before, prisoners of war from conquered lands.

Religious Persecution

Jews and Christians in particular often found themselves on the gladiatorial bill. Crucifixion was a common punishment: the slaves who had joined Spartacus's gladiator army were crucified in their thousands along the Appian Way. Nero also crucified thousands of Christians and set them alight so they could be used as human torches to illuminate the games at night. Tens of thousands of Jewish people ended up in spectacles held by Titus and Vespasian after the Jewish revolt and subsequent fall of Jerusalem in 70 CE.

However, executions aside, Rome was also willing to show clemency and offer its detractors a new life. Most often this took the form of enslavement. Romans considered slavery to be "saving" their enemies from the death they deserved, and this salvation could refer to a single person or an entire culture. Augustus mentions that he was able to "preserve" whole nations in the *Res Gestae Divi Augusti* ("The Things Done by the Divine Augustus"):

> "I often waged war, civil and foreign, on the earth and sea, in the whole wide world, and as victor I spared all the citizens who sought pardon. As for foreign nations, those which I was able to safely forgive, I preferred to preserve than to destroy."

—Augustus, *Res Gestae Divi Augusti*, translated by Thomas Bushnell

Because Romans held the notion that they had done their slaves a favor by saving their lives, it stood to reason that these slaves should be forever in their debt. It was also expected they would constantly show their gratitude to their owners, not only for their lives, but also the food, shelter, and clothing provided

Condemned Criminals

Criminals found guilty of serious crimes also became gladiators, although it is less clear what crimes definitely ended in a *ludus* sentence. Roman writers describe criminals guilty of murder, arson, and temple-robbing becoming gladiators, but others associate the same crimes with the death penalty. It is perhaps likely that condemned criminals with the right fighting qualities ended up as gladiators. By the same token, weaker individuals who would offer up little sport may have been simply sentenced to death.

The place of courts in a slave's sentence changed in the later years of the empire. In the second century CE, Emperor Hadrian passed a law that slaves accused of a crime had to be tried in a court of law and could not be arbitrarily executed by their owner. From the fourth century CE, the sentences of crucifixion and being sent to a *ludus* were abolished altogether.

Right: Hadrian is regarded as one of the five good emperors, a humanist and lover of Greek culture. He also made the beard fashionable among successive Roman emperors.

Facing page: This bas-relief shows gladiators fighting in the Colosseum.

to their owner, the owner also had the right to take that life away. Crucifixion or death by wild beasts were two common punishments for slaves who had seriously displeased their masters. The rest joined those of Rome's outcasts who had been condemned to attend the local *ludus*.

"As for foreign nations, those which I was able to safely forgive, I preferred to preserve than to destroy."

—*Augustus*

GLADIATOR SCHOOL

While many would consider being sent to a *ludus* a fate worse than death, Romans regarded it as a lenient sentence not unlike enslavement. On one hand, gladiators represented the lowest echelons of society who had relinquished their right to live— they were the *infamis*, lower even than actors or prostitutes. On the other hand, gladiators also had a chance to prove their worth and rejoin society. In this sense, a gladiator had greater control over his own destiny than if he were just a slave. If he fought for his life and won, a gladiator might be granted his freedom on the spot.

for them. In turn, Romans saw no problem with disciplining a slave who disobeyed commands. The nature and severity of a punishment always lay at the discretion of the master. There are many examples of owners specifying in their wills that a slave should be prevented from ever attaining their freedom—an act traditionally granted upon the owner's death. Serious disobedience meant death. As a slave owed their life

Left: This sixteenth-century impression shows gladiators fighting in the Roman Forum.

To win his freedom, however, a gladiator would have to fight in the right way. In the great paradox of the gladiatorial games, a gladiator—an *infamis* subhuman who had rebelled against Rome—was also expected to perform according to the virtues that had made Rome great. These were strength (*fortitudo*), training (*disciplina*), firmness (*constantia*), endurance (*patientia*), contempt of death (*contemptus mortis*), love of glory (*amor laudis*), and the desire to win (*cupido victoriae*). By using these qualities, Romans had conquered the known world; by exhibiting them gladiators could earn prizes, fame, freedom, and even respect. Gladiators who behaved like cowards, however, were treated with a vicious contempt. This strange mix of contrary attitudes did not go unnoticed by commentators of the time, such as Tertullian:

> "Next taunts or mutual abuse without any warrant of hate, and applause, unsupported by affection … The perversity of it! They love whom they lower; they despise whom they approve; the art they glorify, the artist they disgrace."

—Tertullian, *De Spectaculis*, translated by S. Thelwall

The Free Gladiator

Considering popular Roman opinion towards the gladiators, it is puzzling to think that large numbers of free men volunteered to become one. As with condemned criminals, slaves, and prisoners of war, it is impossible to calculate the relative figures of free men that entered the arena. However, with the numbers of prisoners of war dropping substantially from the first century CE, some historians estimate that free men made up around half of the gladiators of Rome at that time. It was not only citizens who became gladiators—equestrians, senators, and even emperors also fought in the arena after Augustus made it legal for them to do so.

> *"What gladiator ever gave a sigh? Who ever turned pale? Who ever disgraced himself either in the actual combat, or even when about to die?"*
>
> *—Cicero*

However, apart from the privileged few at the top of Roman society, any free man who opted to join a *ludus* also abandoned all of the privileges they had previously enjoyed. Once a man accepted payment for appearing as a gladiator he joined the ranks of the *infamis* and forever renounced his right to citizenship. Now, his social status was reduced to that of a slave. Like slaves, gladiators were

The Glorious Dregs

The ambivalent attitude the Romans had towards gladiators is neatly summed up by the Republican orator Cicero. He often disparaged his political opponents as gladiators, but in this passage he praises the fighters' stoicism:

Above: Cicero was one of the great Roman orators who tried desperately to defend the ideals of the Republic after the civil war.

"What wounds will the gladiators bear, who are either barbarians, or the very dregs of mankind! How do they, who are trained to it, prefer being wounded to basely avoiding it! How often do they prove that they consider nothing but the giving of satisfaction to their masters or to the people! For when covered with wounds, they send to their masters to learn their pleasure: if it is their will, they are ready to lie down and die. What gladiator, of even moderate reputation, ever gave a sigh? Who ever turned pale? Who ever disgraced himself either in the actual combat, or even when about to die? Who that had been defeated ever drew in his neck to avoid the stroke of death? So great is the force of practice, deliberation and custom! Shall this, then, be done by a Samnite rascal, worthy of his trade; and shall a man born to glory have so soft a part in his soul as not to be able to fortify it by reason and reflection? The sight of the gladiators' combats is by some looked on as cruel and inhuman, and I do not know, as it is at present managed, but it may be so; but when the guilty fought, we might receive by our ears perhaps (but certainly by our eyes we could not) better training to harden us against pain and death."

—Marcus Tullius Cicero, *Cicero's Tusculan Disputations*, translated by C.D. Yonge

Bare-headed Disgrace

During the Roman Republic, the Senate banned aristocrats from fighting as gladiators by saying it did not befit men of their position. While Augustus reversed this legislation at the beginning of the imperial age, Tiberius in turn tried to ban patrician participation when he became emperor. This had very little success. Often, wealthy Romans sidestepped Tiberius's decree by hiding themselves under a helmet. However, not all were so careful. Here, the great Roman satirical poet Juvenal describes the case of Roman aristocrat and tribune Gracchus, who shamed himself by appearing in the arena in 15 CE, during the reign of Tiberius, without a helmet:

"To crown all this [scandal], what is left but the amphitheater? And this disgrace of the city you have as well—Gracchus not fighting as equipped as a *murmillo*, with buckler or falchion (for he condemns—yes, condemns and hates such equipment). Nor does he conceal his face beneath a helmet. See! he wields a trident. When he has cast without effect the nets suspended from his poised right hand, he boldly lifts his uncovered face to the spectators, and, easily to be recognized, flees across the whole arena. We can not mistake the tunic, since the ribbon of gold reaches from his neck, and flutters in the breeze from his high-peaked cap. Therefore, the disgrace, which the *Secutor* had to submit to, in being forced to fight with Gracchus, was worse than any wound."

—Juvenal, *Satire Eight*, translated by G.G. Ramsay

Facing page: A fourth-century-CE mosaic depicts combat between the *secutor* Astyanax and the *retiarius* Kalendio.

Joining a *ludus* was also an option for army veterans returning from abroad who had trouble adapting to civilian life. Although legionaries were granted a parcel of land on retirement, many did not want to be farmers and instead became menial laborers or swords for hire.

Poverty sometimes drove free men to gladiatorial work. An example from the imperial period describes a man needing money to provide a funeral for a dead relative. Another reports a man trying to raise the ransom money to rescue a friend from captivity. Similarly, there are stories of dispossessed aristocrats who had lost or squandered their fortunes and were trying to raise funds by fighting in the arena. While this sounds extreme, many rich equestrians who lost their money found there was very little they could do to generate an income. Some became schoolteachers, or centurions, and others turned to crime. Because upper-class Romans had often been taught to fight as part of their education, becoming a gladiator was a natural choice of career. While proving their worth in the arena as an *infamis* gladiator, disgraced Roman aristocrats could also reemerge into society with some semblance of pride, albeit with a serious shift in status.

Blood Lust

However, other wealthy Romans chose to become gladiators not to win prizes but for the thrill of the experience. Christian apologists such as Tertullian describe a lust for battle that overtook many young, rich patricians in the first century CE when Rome's

completely dependent on their master, usually the *lanista* or *ludus* manager.

There were several reasons for free men to become gladiators. The first was to avoid military service. Commentators from the day suggest that spending a few years as a gladiator was preferable to 20 to 25 years in the army, much of which would undoubtedly have been spent outside the Italian homeland. A man might decide it was better to spend three to five years at a *ludus* trying to win his freedom, or die trying.

ASTYANAX VICIT · KALENDIO O

ASTYANAX · KAI · NEPTIO O

policy of expansion began to slow down. In this case, the writer thought the desire to fight mirrored the moral degeneracy of the Roman elite. There is no question that men at the top of Roman society—like emperors Caligula and Commodus—often enjoyed the violence. However, the participation of the emperors was often met with scorn and derision by patricians and plebeians alike. This was especially so when the emperor gladiators fought with wooden weapons. Commodus, in particular, only ever fought with a wooden *rudis* in the arena.

> ### "Nor does he conceal his face beneath a helmet. See! He wields a trident."
>
> —*Juvenal*

Life at the Ludus

Whatever life the new gladiator had led before, he left it all behind when he entered the gates of the *ludus*. Inside, he would have to swear the *sacramentum gladiatorium*, an oath agreeing "to endure to be burned, to be bound, to be beaten, and to be killed by the sword." The punishment for not swearing to the oath was immediate execution. Free men would then sign a contract stating how long they would fight for, the type of gladiator they would become and how often they would appear in the arena. They then became part of the *familia gladiatoria*, the

gladiatorial family of the *ludus*, which often took the name of the manager or owner. From then on, the gladiator was the property of the *lanista* or *ludus* manager, who was in effect a prison warden who hired out his inmates to whoever was organizing the latest games. Some free men were allowed to sleep outside of the *ludus*, although this did not extend to everyone, and some others chose not to do it.

From 80 CE there were four main *ludi* in Rome that were managed by imperial functionaries, usually highly-paid patricians instead of the usual *lanista*. The handsome remuneration was for two reasons: first, the manager was expected to produce imperial gladiators of the highest quality—good-looking fighters who could go the distance and impress the emperor and crowd alike. Second, being in charge of a gladiatorial school came with a certain risk to life and limb. The revolt of Spartacus had clearly shown that armed gladiators could turn on their masters if given a chance.

GLADIATORIAL TRAINING

The first of Rome's *ludi* were the *Ludus Gallicus* and *Ludus Dacicus*, which originally trained Gallic and Dacian prisoners of war. Another later school, the *Ludus Matutinus* trained the *bestiarii* (animal fighters) and *venatores* (animal hunters). The largest and most important *ludus* was the *Ludus Magnus*, which contained an area large enough to train *equites* (gladiators on horseback) and *essedarii* (gladiators in chariots). The *Ludus Magnus* was connected directly to the Colosseum by a long underground tunnel, so gladiators could enter the complex without being

seen. There were estimated to be more than one hundred *ludi* located across the lands of the Roman Empire, although the exact number is unknown.

On entering the *ludus*, every new gladiator, or *novicius*, was examined by the *ludus* doctor, who was particularly interested in the new man's physical health and appearance. This helped determine whether a *novicius* was up to hours of rigorous training and if their physique would

Above: The ruins of the *Ludus Magnus*, Rome's largest and most important gladiator school.

Facing page: The gladiator's entrance to the Stadium at Aphrodisias, in Aydin province, Turkey.

please the spectators. Any *novicus* considered weak, damaged, or unattractive would be shown the door. Everyone else would be led into their new home, where the rule of the *ludus* was law and the *lanista* reigned like an emperor.

A *ludus* was typically built around a central courtyard where the gladiators trained. The surrounding buildings would include a large kitchen and mess hall, baths, an armory where the weapons were locked away at night, a prison for those gladiators who tried to escape, a medical room, and the gladiators' cells. These small, windowless rooms were usually no larger than 16.4 by 9.8 feet (5 by 3 m) and often shared by two men.

Outside, the training ground was normally oval in shape to imitate the arena floor, and measured around 196.9 by 131.2 feet (60 by 40 m). Along the sides there was raised seating, which, in large *ludi* such as the *Ludus Magnus*, could accommodate up to 3,000 spectators. The spectators included fans, interested aristocrats or gamblers looking for new talent to bet on.

The gladiator's day followed a strict routine. His cell was unlocked at dawn and the first meal of the day taken in the mess hall. The gladiatorial diet earned the fighters the name *hordearii*, or "barley-porridge eaters." The food, often also fed to animals, was designed to provide high levels of energy while also building up fat. Body fat around muscle was considered necessary protection against sword cuts in the arena. Meat was reserved for special occasions, such as the night before a fight. Often this meat came from the beasts slaughtered

Building and Breaking Bodies

Many ancient Roman commentators criticized the high fat content of the barley porridge fed to gladiators. One was the famous medical writer Galen, a doctor who spent time tending to the wounds of gladiators and later became Emperor Marcus Aurelius's personal physician. As Galen writes, his issue was that the fatty diet combined with excessive muscle-building gradually destroyed the bodies of gladiators (here called athletes):

"After this discussion of one of the bodily goods, namely, health, let us pass to the other, how athletes fare on the side of beauty. Not only do they derive none from their profession, but many who have been perfectly proportioned fall into the hands of trainers who develop them beyond measure, overloaded them with flesh and blood, and make them just the opposite …

Above: Galen was Rome's most famous doctor, whose theories dominated Western medicine for centuries after his death.

While athletes pursue their profession their body remains in this dangerous state. When they quit it, they fall into a state even more dangerous. Some die shortly after, others live a little longer, but never reach old age, or if they do they resemble exactly the priests of Homer: 'Limping, deformed and squint-eyed.' In the same way as walls shaken to their foundations by machines of war fall easily on the next attack, athletes, their bodies enfeebled by the jolts they have received, are predisposed to become sick on the least provocation. Their eyes ordinarily sunken, readily become the seat of fluxions; their teeth, so readily injured, fall out. With muscles and tendons frequently torn, their articulations become incapable of resisting strain and readily dislocate."

—Galen, *Exhortation to Study the Arts*, translated by Joseph Walsh

during the *venationes*, and could therefore include such exotic fare as tiger or elephant.

Training Days

After breakfast the *novicius* went to the central courtyard for the training and drills that filled most of his day. To start with, new recruits practiced strokes with a wooden sword (*rudis*) against a 6.6-foot- (2 m)

high pole (*palus*). The *rudis* and all of the practice weapons were twice as heavy as the gladiators' real weapons to help build up strength and stamina.

In time, the *lanista* assigned a gladiator type to each new recruit. They then practiced with the appropriate weapons and armor as taught by a specialist trainer, or *doctor*. *Doctores* were usually ex-gladiators who had lived to tell the tale but were

Facing page: A *retiarius* and *secutor* battle it out in a third-century-CE floor mosaic from a villa in Nennig, Germany.

no longer fit for the arena. The job of a *doctor* was to repeat the same exercises over and over again with their recruit until the movements became instinctive.

Aside from learning to fight as a particular type of gladiator, basic gladiatorial training was similar to that used by the Roman legions. The *rudis* was based on the *gladius*, the sword of the Roman legionary that also gave the gladiators their name. In many of their battle formations, legionaries would lock together their shields and use the *gladius* in a stabbing motion through the gaps. This highly organized method of warfare helped conquer over two and half million square miles of land that made up the Roman Empire. When their battle formations gave way to hand-to-hand combat, legionaries, like gladiators, were expert at identifying and targeting the weakest parts of their opponents' bodies. They also learned that every attack should be blocked by a particular defense and then a specific counterattack.

Vegetius was a fourth-century Roman writer who wrote a military manual outlining the training undertaken by both legionaries and gladiators:

"We are informed by the writings of the ancients that, among their other exercises, they had that of the post [*palus*]. They gave their recruits round bucklers woven with willows, twice as heavy as those used on real service, and wooden swords double the weight of the common ones. They exercised them with these at the post both morning and afternoon. This is an invention of the greatest use, not only to soldiers, but also to gladiators. No man of either profession

ever distinguished himself in the circus or field of battle, who was not perfect in this kind of exercise. Every soldier, therefore, fixed a post firmly in the ground, about the height of six feet. Against this, as against a real enemy, the recruit was exercised with the above mentioned arms, as it were with the common shield and

Left: A representation of a *murmillo* in the arena.

Facing page: Roman legionaries train against the wooden *palus* also used by gladiators in their *ludi*.

"They gave their recruits round bucklers woven with willows, twice as heavy as those used on real service, and wooden swords double the weight of the common ones."

—*Flavius Vegetius Renatus*

Facing page: A seventeenth-century rendering of gladiators fighting at a banquet. In reality, a banquet at the *munera* came after the combat had finished.

"He [Nero] gave the gladiator Spiculus properties and residences equal to those of men who had celebrated triumphs."

—Suetonius

sword, sometimes aiming at the head or face, sometimes at the sides, at others endeavouring to strike at the thighs or legs. He was instructed in what manner to advance and retire, and in short how to take every advantage of his adversary; but was thus above all particularly cautioned not to lay himself open to his antagonist while aiming his stroke at him … They were likewise taught not to cut but to thrust with their swords. For the Romans not only made a jest of those who fought with the edge of that weapon, but always found them an easy conquest. A stroke with the edges, though made with ever so much force, seldom kills, as the vital parts of the body are defended both by the bones and armor. On the contrary, a stab, though it penetrates but two inches, is generally fatal."
—Flavius Vegetius Renatus, *The Military Institutions of the Romans*, translated by John Clarke

The *palus* was not just a training instrument but also a symbol for the best fighters at a *ludus*. Any gladiator who had beaten his opponent in the arena could call himself a *veteranus*. The top *veteranus* within each gladiator school was the one who had won the most contests and would therefore be honored with the title *primus palus* (first pole). The second best was called *secundus palus* (second pole), and so on. Rivalry was actively encouraged at *ludi* and competition between gladiators was fierce. For this reason, the different types of gladiators were kept segregated from each other when they were not

in training. A type of gladiator called a *murmillo* was often pitted against a *thraex* in the arena but the two were kept apart outside it.

Comrade-in-Arms

Despite this policy of segregation, however, bonds were formed between gladiators in the *ludus*. These relationships must have been a strange mix of competition and camaraderie. One evening two gladiators eating dinner in the same *ludus* mess hall could next day be trying to kill each other in the arena. The survivor of this encounter might then end up burying his adversary. This is because the gladiators of each *ludus* often formed a type of trade union called a *collegia*, which tried to protect the rights of its members. These *collegia* would take responsibility for gladiatorial funerals and forwarding his effects to the appropriate family member in the event of death.

For most gladiators the chances of bequeathing a fortune to their relatives was small. Gladiators were grouped into different price bands and would cost a spectacle organizer, or *editor*, between 1,000 and 15,000 sestertii to fight in the arena. Most of this fee went into the *lanista*'s pocket, with the gladiator themselves only taking a cut of the money if they won. At best, a gladiator could expect around 20 percent, or perhaps 25 percent for a free man. On the other hand, a seasoned *veteranus* who had won his freedom could expect to make good money if he returned to the arena.

A freed gladiator was called a *rudiarius*, after being awarded the wooden training *rudis* as a

Fighting the Odds

Tomb inscriptions and gladiatorial advertising from Rome and Pompeii show us that gladiators did not always have to win a fight to come away with their lives. These records describe gladiators who had survived 30 bouts in the arena, but had only won half of them. Other information suggests that a gladiator who won more than five fights often became popular enough with the crowd to have the thumbs turned in his favor.

Tomb inscriptions show the ages of different gladiators at death and how many fights they had won. One inscription from Padua records a man losing his life at the age of 21 after five fights and four years in a *ludus*. Another inscription from Sicily shows a gladiator dying after 34 fights, 21 victories, nine draws and four defeats. An inscription from Rome reports a gladiator retired after 20 years in the *Ludis Caesaris* and 19 victories, and later died a free man at 48.

While there is no such thing as average or statistical odds for gladiators, some estimates suggest each one had a three in five chance of surviving every bout. These odds strengthened as the gladiator become more experienced, but some writers report the average gladiator was killed within the first two years of their five-year contract. Gladiators were often expected to fight at two or three *munera* a year, although there are records of one gladiator fighting every day for nine days in a row at Trajan's games. He was then granted his freedom by the emperor.

Above: A gladiator tomb in the ancient city of Hierapolis, Turkey.

Left: The central training yard in the gladiator *ludus* in the city of Pompeii.

symbol of his freedom and allowed to walk from the arena. This was rare but a great crowd-pleaser when it happened. By the same token, a *rudiarius* returning to the arena was likely to draw many spectators and a hefty fee. However, those new recruits fighting at the other end of the scale could expect only a few coins for a victorious bout.

Occasionally a gladiator who had won the favor of the crowd and emperor would be rewarded with rich prizes. Nero, never one to worry about the bill, was known to be particularly generous. According to Suetonius: "He gave the gladiator Spiculus properties and residences equal to those of men who had celebrated triumphs."

After the Arena
Lanistae made a high income from their gladiators but were regarded as little more than pimps and

butchers by the Roman public. It was important for a *lanista* to keep his best gladiators in top fighting form so they could appear in the arena over and over again. On the other hand, a *lanista* would be fully reimbursed by the *editor* for any gladiator killed during their spectacle. In this sense, it was win-win for the *lanista* whatever the outcome.

While *lanistae* often retired to a comfortable villa outside Rome, the retirement options for most gladiators were less attractive. Few of those who were not free men made enough to buy their freedom, find a wife, and live a normal life outside the *ludus*. All gladiators, regardless of their background, were considered *infamis*, and this tag remained with them until death.

A common source of employment was as a bodyguard for a wealthy aristocrat. This often occurred during the Republican period, and Nero and Caligula were both known to have incorporated ex-gladiators into their security retinues. Another option was to open a business. Like modern-day prizefighters, a restaurant or bar owned by a famous ex-gladiator appealed to star-struck patrons. Frequenting such premises gave them the chance to rub up against a star of the arena—until, of course, the sheen wore off.

For the many ex-gladiators who found it difficult to adjust to life outside the arena, there was always the chance to return as a *rudiarius*. A famous example of a returning gladiator is Flamma, who was awarded the *rudis* four times, but every time chose to remain a gladiator. His gravestone in Sicily bears the following inscription:

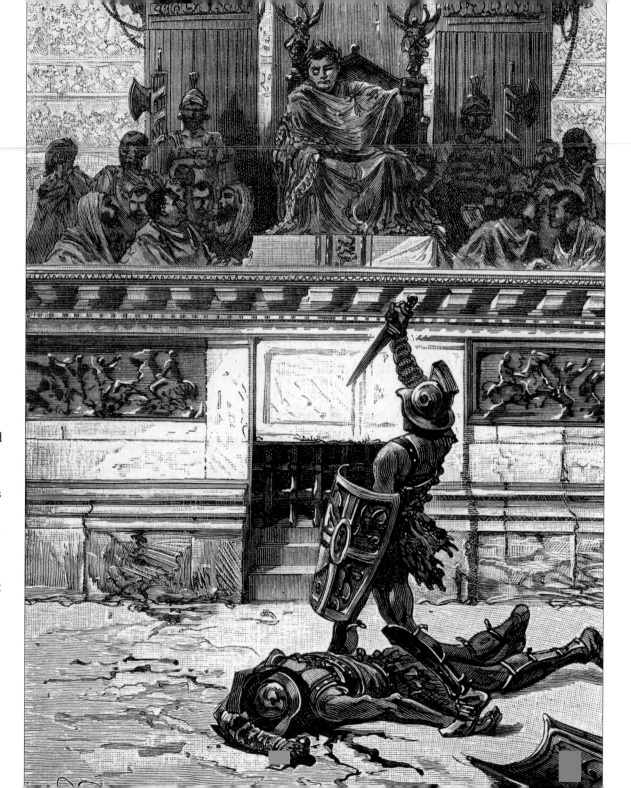

FLAMMA, SECUTOR, LIVED 30 YEARS, FOUGHT 34 TIMES, WON 21 TIMES, FOUGHT TO A DRAW 9 TIMES, DEFEATED 4 TIMES, A SYRIAN BY NATIONALITY. DELICATUS MADE THIS FOR HIS DESERVING COMRADE-IN-ARMS.

It is likely the *rudiarii* are the men described by the poet Horace, who once wrote that it was possible for gladiators to retire rich men to a rural estate. On one occasion, Emperor Tiberius was known to have offered a purse of 100,000 sesterces to a *rudiarius* to tempt him back into the arena. A last fight for serious money was a difficult offer to refuse. However, a wise *rudiarius* knew that his last fight was potentially as dangerous as his first.

A common option for retired gladiators was to return to the *ludus* as a *doctor*. This enabled them to stay close to the action, pass their valuable fighting knowledge on to those who needed it, and provide a neat propaganda tool for the *lanista*. It showed new recruits that it was possible not only to survive their

Gladiator Suicide

While some gladiators fought their way up to *primus palus*, winning acclaim, freedom, and a healthy retirement purse, they were in the minority. For many, the *ludus* was the last stop before a violent and anonymous end on the sands of the arena as a hostile crowd bayed for their blood. The pressure and shame was too much for some who chose the fastest exit possible, as Seneca writes:

> "Lately a gladiator, who had been sent forth to the morning exhibition, was being conveyed in a cart along with the other prisoners; nodding as if he were heavy with sleep, he let his head fall over so far that it was caught in the spokes; then he kept his body in position long enough to break his neck by the revolution of the wheel. So he made his escape by means of the very wagon which was carrying him to his punishment."

But taking one's life was not something easily done, especially for a new recruit kept in chains at all times outside of the training yard. It was not uncommon for these inexperienced gladiators to quickly hit breaking point, and so they were closely watched. For this reason, opportunities to take one's life were few and far between, and suicide required a desperate level of initiative. Seneca describes one such case:

> "For example, there was lately in a training-school for wild-beast gladiators a German, who was making ready for the morning exhibition; he withdrew in order to relieve himself—the only thing which he was allowed to do in secret and without the presence of a guard. While so engaged, he seized the stick of wood, tipped with a sponge, which was devoted to the vilest uses, and stuffed it, just as it was, down his throat; thus he blocked up his windpipe, and choked the breath from his body. That was truly to insult death!"

—Seneca, *Moral Letters to Lucilius*, translated by Richard M. Gummere

Right: Seneca was an aristocrat, philosopher, and dramatist who tutored Nero. The emperor later made Seneca commit suicide for a supposed plot on his life.

Right: A marble relief of the female gladiators Amazonia and Achillea. Their fight reportedly ended in a draw and a *missio* for both.

gladiatorial contract but also to lead a life outside the arena afterwards.

Leaving the *ludus* was a dream shared by every gladiator competing for his life; most, however, did not get out. If they survived and won their freedom, they often found themselves institutionalized and unable to cope with life outside the *ludus*. Many squandered the money they had and then ended up back at the *ludus* to fight, train, or pick up odd jobs here and there wherever they could. Many were left destitute and begging on the street, before suffering the ignominious end of so many of Rome's underclass—burned on an anonymous funeral pyre or slung into an unmarked mass grave.

FEMALE GLADIATORS

With the tradition of *munera* spanning several hundred years of Roman history, it is perhaps no surprise that women fought in the arena. Like their male counterparts, these gladiators included free and noble women alongside those forced to fight against their will. While it seems remarkable that an aristocratic Roman woman would demean herself by appearing alongside the *infamis* in the arena, it is possible they escaped this label by not accepting payment for the contest.

The appearance of women must have caused a certain amount of consternation—in 11 CE Augustus put restrictions on female gladiators that

forbade any free woman under 20 from appearing in the arena. Tiberius passed another decree in 19 CE banning aristocratic Roman women of any age from fighting as a gladiator.

However, these imperial commands seemed to have little lasting effect and the trend of female gladiators continued well into the days of empire. Nero's tribute games to his mother featured women not only fighting as gladiators, but also driving chariots and hunting animals. Emperor Domitian, who loved novelty in the arena, arranged for torch-lit nighttime fights between female gladiators and dwarfs.

Two of the most famous female gladiators of the Roman Empire—Achillea and Amazonia—fought in Asia Minor. A marble relief depicting the two women in combat was found in modern Turkey, and dates from between the first and second century CE. The gladiators are shown wearing loincloths instead of tunics and armed with *gladii*, large shields, leg greaves, and *manicae* (arm protectors). Their helmets have been discarded nearby onto the arena floor, perhaps to show the audience that they were not men.

Although the fight between Achillea and Amazonia was considered important enough to be the subject of an expensive commissioned artwork, the sight of female gladiators offended the sensibilities of many male Romans. This was certainly true of Emperor Septimius Severus, who banned female gladiators altogether in 200 CE. The masculine position is scornfully summed up by Juvenal:

Right: Emperor Septimius Severus was a despotic military ruler who founded a personal dynasty and banned females from fighting as gladiators.

"Why need I tell of the purple wraps and the wrestling-oils used by women? Who has not seen one of them smiting a stump, piercing it through and through with a foil, lunging at it with a shield, and going through all the proper motions?—a matron truly qualified to blow a trumpet at the Floralia! Unless, indeed, she is nursing some further ambition in her bosom, and is practicing for the real arena. What modesty can you expect in a woman who wears a helmet, abjures her own sex, and delights in feats of strength? Yet she would not choose to be a man, knowing the superior joys of womanhood. What a fine thing for a husband, at an auction of his wife's effects, to see her belt and armlets and plumes put up for sale, with a gaiter that covers half the left leg; or if she fight another sort of battle, how charmed you will be to see your young wife disposing of her greaves! Yet these are the women who find the thinnest of thin robes too hot for them; whose delicate flesh is chafed by the finest of silk tissue. See how she pants as she goes through her prescribed exercises; how she bends under the weight of her helmet; how big and coarse are the bandages which enclose her haunches; and then laugh when she lays down her arms and shows herself to be a woman!
—Juvenal, *Satire Six*, translated by G.G. Ramsay

Sex in the Cells

Although the numbers of females fighting in the arena were small, the gladiatorial games and their performers had a profound effect on many other women who watched them. Handsome and heroic gladiators often won the hearts of the crowd and achieved the kind of acclaim that film stars enjoy today. These gladiators were admired by men and loved by women. The poet Martial describes the glories of one such gladiator, Hermes:

"Hermes, the age's delight to the Sons of Mars; Hermes, schooled in all weapons; Hermes, gladiator and trainer both; Hermes, the confusion and terror of his own school … Hermes, the darling and passion of gladiators' women; Hermes, proud with the warrior's spear."
—Martial, *Epigrams*, translated by Walter C.A. Ker

In shorter and coarser scrawls, graffiti artists describe the effects certain gladiators could have on Roman women. Inscriptions found on the walls of Pompeii include: "Celadus makes the girls swoon" (*Celadus, suspirium puellarum*) and "Cresces the Netter of young girls by night" (*Cresces retiarius puparum nocturnarum*).

It was not uncommon for the *lanista* of a *ludus* to send a slave to a gladiator's cell as a reward for fighting well. For a price, infatuated free women could also enjoy similar access. Among the ranks of female visitors were those from the Roman aristocracy.

Juvenal recounts the love of senatorial wife Eppia for the gladiator Sergius. Eppia gives up her "soft downy pillows" and "wailing children" to follow Sergius and his touring *familia gladiatoria*

Above: According to contemporary sources, even the sight of gladiators was said to have an intoxicating effect on many Roman women.

to Alexandria in Egypt. Juvenal finds this curious for two reasons—firstly because of the torturous sea journey to Egypt, which was avoided if at all possible, and secondly because Sergius was not an attractive man:

> "And what were the youthful charms which captivated Eppia? What did she see in him to allow herself to be called 'a she-Gladiator'? Her dear Sergius had already begun to shave; a wounded arm gave promise of a discharge, and there were sundry deformities in his face: a scar caused by the helmet, a huge wen upon his nose, a nasty humour always trickling from his eye. But then he was a gladiator! It is this that transforms these fellows into Hyacinths! It was this that she preferred to children and to country, to sister and to husband. What these women love is the sword."

—Juvenal, *Satire Six*, translated by G.G. Ramsay

Another story describes Faustina, the wife of Emperor Marcus Aurelius, who became instantly inflamed by a gladiator she had seen in a procession. She was so overcome with her lust for the gladiator that she admitted her passion to Marcus Aurelius. The emperor consulted the priests, who advised that the gladiator should be killed so Faustina could bathe in his blood and then have sex with her husband.

Faustina carried out the prescription, which seemed to work, as her love abated afterwards. But the child born from the bloody union of that night turned out to be heir apparent Commodus.

Commodus was one of the most infamous of Rome's emperors, who, according to senator Cassius Dio:

> "… was born a gladiator, not really a prince; for afterwards as emperor he fought almost a thousand gladiatorial bouts before the eyes of the people, as shall be related in his life. This story is considered plausible, as a matter of fact, for the reason that the son of so virtuous a prince had habits worse than any trainer of gladiators, any play-actor, any fighter in the arena, anything brought into existence from the offscourings of all dishonor and crime."

—Cassius Dio, *Roman History*, translated by Earnest Cary

COMMODUS (161–192 CE)

Marcus Aurelius Commodus Antoninus Augustus was an emperor who could well have taken his lead from the degenerate Julio-Claudian emperors of the early empire. Like Nero, Commodus thrived under an emperorship that was apparently free from consequence. Also like Nero, he indulged himself in tyranny, turpitude, and familial murder. And like Caligula, Commodus's love for the games was such that he appeared in the arena as a gladiator.

Commodus was born to Marcus Aurelius, the last of the so-called "Five Good Emperors," and ruled as co-emperor with his father until his death in 180 CE. On hearing the news of his father's demise, Commodus left his soldiers to continue his campaign on the Danube and rode

Facing page: This nineteenth-century painting of a gladiatorial contest at a dinner party shows the women of the household gathered round the victor.

Below: Faustina was the daughter of Emperor Antoninus Pius and wife to Emperor Marcus Aurelius, her cousin. She gave birth to Commodus, the emperor gladiator.

back to the sunnier climes of Rome. On his return, Commodus awarded himself a triumph, negotiated a peace with the Danubian tribes, and settled into royal life in the capital.

In a familiar path already trodden by corrupt emperors, Commodus preferred earthly pursuits to affairs of the state. To keep the imperial coffers full, he sold political offices to the highest bidders and agreed to let various hostile Germanic tribes live within Roman borders in exchange for cash. These actions led directly to a series of plots against Commodus's life, including one planned by the Senate and his sister, Lucilla. When he discovered the conspiracy, Commodus had Lucilla and her fellow conspirators executed and took over managing the empire in the style of a tyrant.

Cassius Dio, a senator during Commodus's rule, accused Commodus of turning Rome "from a kingdom of gold to one of rust and iron." Modern historians consider Commodus's reign to herald the beginning of the end of the Roman Empire. Ironically, Rome's borders were all but conflict-free while Commodus was emperor. But the decline of the empire did not begin at its outer reaches; instead the rot started at its core—Rome.

In the first of many self-serving actions, Commodus devalued the Roman currency and raised funds for his increasingly extravagant lifestyle by extorting money from the aristocracy. Some were blackmailed with charges of treason and had to pay Commodus to stay alive; many nobles were simply executed for their fortunes. Dio describes his emperor:

"Commodus, taking a respite from his amusements and sports, turned to murder and was killing off the prominent men … Commodus was guilty of many unseemly deeds, and killed a great many people."
—Cassius Dio, *Roman History*, translated by Earnest Cary

While Commodus showed he was willing to kill anyone at any time, he won the respect of the *Populus Romanus* by holding numerous spectacles and then taking part as a gladiator. Fair and athletic, Commodus would dress in the skin of a lion, carry a club and liken himself to the mythical demigod Hercules. In the arena he drove chariots, hunted animals and was regarded as a crack shot with spear or bow, as Dio describes:

"Commodus devoted most of his life to ease and to horses and to combats of wild beasts and of men. In fact, besides all that he did in private, he often slew in public large numbers of men and beasts as well. For example, all alone with his own hands, he dispatched five hippopotami together with two elephants on two successive days; and he also killed rhinoceroses and a camelopard [giraffe]."
—Cassius Dio, *Roman History*, translated by Earnest Cary

Commodus actively referred to himself as one of the greatest gladiators who had ever lived, and littered Rome with personal effigies. He ordered the head removed from the Colossus of Nero and replaced

with his own likeness. He adorned the statue with a club, lion skin and bronze lion at its feet, and fitted it with the inscription: "the only left-handed fighter to conquer twelve times one thousand men." Commodus then officially renamed Rome *Colonia Lucia Annia Commodiana*, or "Colony of Commodus."

But the emperor's contests in the arena were farcical at best. Here, Commodus used a wooden sword to fight his opponent, who would obviously not consider harming his emperor. Outside the arena, Commodus turned his palace into a gladiatorial training ground. During his palace sessions, Commodus would use a steel blade against his opponents, unlike his bouts in the ring:

"… he used to contend as a gladiator; in doing this at home he managed to kill a man now and

Above: A coin bearing the head of Commodus, who co-ruled with his father Marcus Aurelius before becoming emperor upon his death.

Facing page: Emperor Marcus Aurelius was a Stoic philosopher who ruled with self-restraint and respect for others, virtues that were entirely abandoned by his heir Commodus.

Left: A statue of Commodus dressed as Hercules: the emperor liked to compare himself to the demigod.

Facing page: A romantic rendering of Commodus killing a panther with an arrow. Despite avoiding gladiatorial combat with real weapons in the arena, the emperor was a crack shot with the bow.

then, and in making close passes with others, as if trying to clip off a bit of their hair, he sliced off the noses of some, the ears of others, and sundry features of still others."
—Cassius Dio, *Roman History*, translated by Earnest Cary

Colosseum Costume Changes

On the day of the games, Commodus's lion skin and club were carried before the litter that bore him to the Colosseum. The emperor then proceeded through a series of costume changes. He would arrive in a white silk toga to greet the senators, then don a purple robe and gold crown to sit in the imperial box before entering the arena barefoot in a simple tunic to fight. The lion skin and club, when not in use, sat on a gilded chair in the royal box.

It was from his box that Commodus would participate in the first event of the day—the animal hunts. On one particularly successful morning, the emperor killed 100 bears by throwing spears from the balustrade. This activity was made easier as the arena had been split into four parts with dividing walls, but Commodus's efforts left him exhausted. After drinking down a measure of wine from a

cup shaped like a club, Commodus looked to the audience, who on cue shouted: "Long life to you!"

The emperor often introduced the afternoon event, the gladiator fights, by adding himself to the bill. He would enter the arena dressed as a *secutor* and sometimes let the audience choose his opponent—although it was no surprise that Commodus won all of his contests. He rewarded himself handsomely for these bouts, taking a fee of one million sesterces. This was a colossal sum, especially for a working gladiator, who at best could command 15,000 sesterces for his services.

After Commodus's dalliance in the arena he dressed as the god Mercury and retired to the royal box to watch the real gladiator fights. These were observed with keen interest by their "gladiator" emperor, who would encourage the fighters to indulge in increased levels of brutality from his imperial vantage point. On one occasion when some of the victorious gladiators hesitated in finishing off their defeated opponents, an incensed Commodus ordered that all of the combatants be shackled together and fight until none were left standing.

At another time, Commodus commanded that

Above: Here, Commodus joins the *pompa* during one of his many appearances as a gladiator in the Colosseum.

Facing page: Gladiators greet the emperor in his imperial box as part of the *pompa*, a procession that preceded their combat.

Right: Commodus would slaughter harmless herbivores, such as ostriches, with a bow and arrow, as well as more savage beasts, such as bears, by throwing spears.

every man in the city missing a foot to disease or misfortune be rounded up and brought to the Colosseum. Here, they were fastened around the knees with ropes fashioned as serpents and given sponges to throw at Commodus. Dressed as Hercules, Commodus then battered the men to death with his club, calling the spectacle the "slaying of the giants."

After each of Commodus's events the crowd was obliged to shout out: "Thou art lord and thou art first, of all men most fortunate. Victor thou art, and victor thou shalt be; from everlasting, Amazonian, thou art victor." But people missed out on the emperors' later events as they were too scared to attend. After a while, nobody was safe when Commodus was at large. At one stage many stayed away from the Colosseum when a rumor circulated that Commodus was preparing to shoot a few of the spectators in a reenactment of Hercules's sixth task, the killing of the Stymphalian birds. No one believed Commodus was above such an act, least of all the senators, who were in constant fear of death. One of these was Cassius Dio, who recounted a particularly close shave:

"And here is another thing that he did to us senators which gave us every reason to look for our death. Having killed an ostrich and cut off his head, he came up to where we were sitting, holding the head in his left hand and in his

right hand raising aloft his bloody sword; and though he spoke not a word, yet he wagged his head with a grin, indicating that he would treat us in the same way. And many would indeed have perished by the sword on the spot, for laughing at him (for it was laughter rather than indignation that overcame us), if I had not chewed some laurel leaves, which I got from my garland, myself, and persuaded the others who were sitting near me to do the same, so that in the steady movement of our arms we might conceal the fact that we were laughing."

In the end, Commodus shared the same fate as many of Rome's tyrannical emperors. His undoing was to announce that he would inaugurate the year 193 CE as a consul dressed as a *secutor* from the cell of a gladiator. His mistress, Marcia, tried to talk him out of the notion, but in reaction Commodus ordered her execution. On discovering her death sentence, Marcia and the commander of the Praetorian Guard tried to poison Commodus. When this failed, they hired a wrestler to strangle the emperor in his bath. The Senate then declared Commodus an enemy of the state, ordered his statues torn down and the name of Rome restored to the city.

Left: *The Death of the Emperor Commodus* by artist Fernand Pelez. Commodus's mistress Marcia watches his assassination from the shadows. Marcia had pleaded with the emperor to abandon his plans to inaugurate the new year as a gladiator. In response he ordered her execution.

Types of Gladiators

The gladiators of the Roman Republic modeled themselves on the tribal warriors its legions had defeated in battle. By showcasing the weapons and armor of these conquered people in the arena, the public was reminded of Rome's victories over its foreign enemies. Over time these gladiators evolved into the recognizable fighters we associate with the games today.

Most of what we know about the appearance, equipment, and combat styles of gladiators comes from the Roman Empire between the first and third century CE. It was Augustus who first gave the games an organized structure and a classification system for the fighters themselves. Imperial gladiators fought in clearly defined categories, called *armaturae*—they carried particular armaments and often faced specific opponents in the arena.

The codification of the games was a marked departure from the *munera* held by the grieving families of wealthy Republicans. Unlike the later

empire, there are virtually no written records about *munera* fighters from the early Republic. Instead, most of what we know comes from the fourth-century-BCE tomb paintings found in Paestum, Campania. Regarded as the earliest representation of gladiatorial fighters, these frescos show men in single combat, some naked and others dressed in loincloths and tunics. The fighters carry spears, lances, and the large round shield used by the ancient Greek hoplites. Their helmets, also based on the Greek style, were almost certainly made from sheets of beaten bronze.

The next pictorial evidence of *munera* and those who fought at them does not appear again until the late Republic. Reliefs from this period show contests between naked fighters and others wearing loincloths held in place by broad bronze belts. These gladiators are shown wearing Hellenistic-style helmets with the same curved brim used by Roman legionaries at that time.

Facing page: It is a popular misconception that gladiators greeted the emperor with "Hail Caesar, we who are about to die salute you" before combat. This happened only once in recorded history, during a *naumachia* held by Claudius.

Right: A third-century-CE terracotta figure of a *secutor* gladiator.

SAMNITE

EQUITES

THRACES

DIMACHERUS

MIRMILLO

RETIARIUS

SECUTOR

Some of the fighters are protected by a padded arm guard called a *manica* and a rectangular breastplate attached by straps at the back. Greaves, or shin guards, are also shown. The lances and spears pictured in the Paestum frescos have now been replaced by the short, stabbing sword made famous by the Roman legionaries—the *gladius hispaniensis*, or Spanish sword.

MAIN GLADIATOR TYPES

The army's tremendous success in defeating Rome's neighbors in Italy and abroad led to the first three identifiable gladiator categories during the late Republican era: the *samnis* or Samnite, *gallus* or Gaul, and *thraex*, Thracian. The *samnis* is the type of gladiator mentioned most commonly in the literature from this time. The Samnites were originally a tribal people based in the Italian region of Campania, who fought a long series of wars against Rome in the third and fourth centuries BCE. It is therefore no surprise that gladiators based on the Samnite warrior were used during early *munera* in Campania, the heartland of Roman gladiatorial contests. Probably somewhat embellished from the original Samnite model for effect, the *samnis* gladiator was equipped with a large rectangular shield, a short 20 inches (50 centimeters) sword, a broad leather belt, a visored helmet with a plume and one leg greave. The category of *samnis* faded from view during the early imperial period, and was replaced by the similarly armed *hoplomachus* and *secutor*.

The fate of the Samnite people also befell the various tribes of Celtic Gaul, who then became the inspiration for the *gallus* gladiator. The Thracians similarly became the model for the *thraex*. It is probable that both the Gaulish and Thracian warriors were forced to fight in the arena themselves, before their weapons and fighting styles were appropriated for use by trained gladiators. There is no record of the *gallus* beyond the Republican period and it is likely this type of gladiator went on to form the basis of the later *murmillo*. It is thought in his time the *gallus* carried a large rectangular shield, fought with a sword and wore a helmet and one greave.

The *thraex* made his appearance in the first century after Rome conquered the Thracians and made Thrace—present-day Bulgaria with parts of Romania, Greece, and Turkey—a permanent Roman client state. Unlike the *samnis* and *gallus*, the *thraex* retained its place as a popular gladiatorial type beyond the Republican period—it lasted throughout the imperial age and up until the last spectacles of Rome.

Although the *thraex* kept his ethnic name for the duration of gladiatorial history, most Republican gladiators gave way to rebranded versions of themselves for the imperial age. This rebranding included being given a new name that held no cultural overtones. The Romans believed that continually referring

Facing page: Illustration of various gladiatorial types. The first gladiators were based on the warriors of conquered people, such as the Samnites.

Below: A marble funerary relief showing a Thracian horseman.

to parts of their new population as gladiators might unnecessarily upset the delicate process of integration. So, after a suitable period of parading a conquered people's warriors—or the gladiatorial models based on them—in the arena, rebranding took place in the name of assimilation. It would have been wholly unfitting for ethnic groups such as the Gauls and Samnites to be presented as outsiders during the time of Augustus, as its people had been living as Roman citizens for generations. So the *gallus* became the *murmillo*, or sea fish.

The gladiators featured in the following pages were the most popular during the imperial age, when the fighters were organized into standardized categories. It is consequently also the period from Roman history that gives us the most information about gladiator types and their weaponry and armor. Notably, much of this equipment was found intact during the excavation of the city of Pompeii in the eighteenth century.

Provocator

The *provocator*, or "challenger," appeared during the Roman Republican period and continued throughout the imperial age. An early reference to the *provocator* is made by Republican orator Cicero in a diatribe about gladiators that included the *samnis* and *eques*. As the *provocator* survived for many centuries of Roman history, his likeness is depicted in several reliefs, mostly dating from the imperial period. These show that the *provocator*'s helmet evolved over the later years of the empire, although his armor remained largely unchanged.

As this armor would only ever have weighed up to 33 pounds (15 kg), the *provocator* was considered a medium-armed gladiator.

The *provocator* wore a heavy loincloth, a broad metal belt, one knee-level greave, and a *manica* covering the forearm of his sword arm. Protecting the gladiator's chest was a *cardiophylax*, a Greek word for a partial breastplate that is the hallmark of this type of fighter. Usually the *cardiophylax* was made of a piece of solid, rectangular metal, although a crescent-shaped breastplate was also used and occasionally one made from metal plates. The *cardiophylax* was sometimes decorated with images of mythical creatures and usually fastened by leather straps at the back. The *provocator* was also protected by a medium-sized rectangular shield and he carried a short sword with a straight blade.

The *provocator*'s helmet was one of the most interesting pieces of his kit. In a relief from the Augustan period, two dueling *provocatores* are shown wearing the imperial Gallic helmet. This was specially designed for legionaries of the late Republic and combined both Roman and Celtic features.

Notably, the Roman influence can be seen through the feathers adorning the sides of the helmet, a tradition that harked from the early Republic. These side feathers were abandoned during the imperial period and the helmet was updated with a round, lattice-hole visor for the eyes. The helmet's brims were also constructed at a lower-facing angle and lengthened to make it more streamlined and to give greater protection to the neck.

Left: Detail of gladiatorial combat from a sarcophagus found in the ancient city of Ephesus, modern-day Turkey.

Facing page: A bronze figurine of a *thraex* gladiator.

Eques

The *eques* was another gladiator who lasted beyond the Republican period and into the imperial age without having a makeover or a change of name. Described as horsemen, the *equites* are most often depicted in reliefs from the Republican era as fighting on the ground with a sword. This is because *equites* began their contests on horseback but then either dismounted or were thrown onto the arena floor. To start with, an *eques* would ride into the arena on a white horse armed with a spear or lance.

Like the *provocator*, the *eques* only ever fought against the same type of gladiator as himself, and for this reason a battle between two *equites* was not dissimilar to a medieval joust. The *eques* wore a crestless, brimmed helmet that was often

Provocator in Combat

A *provocator* was almost always pitted against another *provocator* in the arena. Because this meant a bout between two medium-armed gladiators, contests were short, energetic and featured quick, darting movements, and lightning-fast counterattacks. The *provocator* fought barefoot, which enabled the gladiator to be light and agile and use sliding motions across the sandy floor to approach and retreat from his opponent. Being without boots also allowed a *provocator* to feel anything untoward underfoot, such as nets and trapdoors.

A *provocator*'s large shield was used in both defense and attack. Made from oak and reinforced with iron, the shield's central grip and metal dome at the front could be crashed against the adversary to disarm or knock him off his feet. Later *provocator* shields from the imperial age often had sharp metal edges at the top and bottom. This allowed the shield to be used as a heavy cutting edge to slice feet or behead an opponent lying on the ground.

A *provocator*'s helmet gave his head, and, in the later imperial age, his neck, almost complete protection. However, it also greatly restricted his field of vision and made breathing difficult. Because of the high-energy nature of a bout between two *provocatores*, helmets quickly became stuffy and left the gladiators' heads drenched with sweat. The small apertures in the *provocator*'s helmet meant he was trained never to take his eyes off his opponent. He would shuffle forward slowly, with shield pointing face-on at his adversary. Keeping his *gladius* blade partially obscured by his shield, the *provocator* would make fast attacks before drawing back behind his shield. Every gladiator knew a successful stab was only ever around half an inch from an opponent's major artery or organ, and stabbing thrusts were always favored over a cutting or hacking motion. For this reason, the parry and blow techniques of later medieval knights were seldom witnessed at a gladiator contest.

Right: The *provocator* gladiator is shown wearing a helmet with brims bent downwards to protect the neck.

decorated with a feather on either side. He carried a round, medium-sized shield called a *parma equestris* that was also used by the horsemen of the Republican cavalry. An *eques* did not wear greaves but instead sometimes protected his legs with leather wrappings. Early reliefs show *equites* in

jerkins made from scaled armor. In the later period these appear to have been replaced by bright tunics, differently colored so the spectators could tell the combatants apart.

An *eques* protected his sword arm with a thick *manica* and he carried a spear or lance around

Above: This seventeenth-century painting shows gladiators and soldiers in a processional *pompa*.

Above: An illustration of two *murmillo*-style gladiators showing how a well-placed cut could put a combatant out of commission.

8 feet 2 inches (2.5 m) long. When this weapon was discarded for further combat on the ground, the *eques* used the medium-length *gladius* sword, which was also used by Roman legionaries. As his armor weighed no more than 12kg (26lb), the *eques* was considered a lightly-armed gladiator.

Thraex

The *thraex* was one of the most popular Roman gladiators. Originally based on the Thracian prisoners of war during the Republican period, the *thraex* of the imperial age bore little resemblance to his warrior namesake. A *thraex* used similar equipment to the *hoplomachus* and the two gladiators were often mistaken for one another.

The *thraex*'s medium-sized rectangular shield set him apart from the *hoplomachus*. Constructed from wood, covered with leather, and reinforced with metal edges, this "*parmula*" shield was distinctive but ineffective in protecting the *thraex*'s lower body. For this reason, the *thraex* wore padded wrappings around his legs with tall greaves over the top, and bolstered this defense with a padded *manica* on his dominant arm.

The most recognizable part of a *thraex*'s armor was his brimmed helmet, which featured a crest formed into the shape of a griffin. The griffin was a mythological creature with the body of a lion and head and wings of an eagle that was commonly associated with Nemesis, the Greek goddess of retribution. The *thraex*'s griffin crest was further adorned with a bright plumage of bird's feathers. At times a single feather was also attached to either side of a *thraex*'s helmet.

The *thraex*'s primary weapon was the slightly curved *sica* sword, the curvature of which varied over the centuries. With armor weighing up to 40 pounds (18 kg), the *thraex* was considered a heavily-armed gladiator who was often pitted against a similarly-armed opponent—the *murmillo*.

Left: Like Roman legionaries, gladiators were trained to target the most vulnerable places on their opponents' bodies, as this bas-relief shows.

Murmillo

The *murmillo* was the gladiator who replaced the *gallus*, the Republican-age fighter who needed to be renamed after the Gauls became integrated into Roman society. *Murmillo* means "sea fish" and the gladiator's broad-brimmed, visored helmet was fitted with a large crest in the shape of a dorsal fin and adorned with feathers. Two single feathers were also often attached to the side of the helmet. While most of the *murmillo* helmets were made from bronze, some were steel-plated to give the impression of fish scales.

Aside from his helmet, a *murmillo* would wear no other armor in the arena except for a long, folded loincloth with a broad, ornamented belt, a padded *manica* on his sword arm, thick leg wrappings, and one knee-high greave. Unlike the *thraex*, the *murmillo* was protected by the large, 3 feet 3 inches (1 m) high rectangular shield used by the imperial Roman legionaries. The *murmillo's* single weapon was the *gladius* sword, which was sometimes attached to the gladiator by a cord so it could always be retrieved.

With weapons and armor weighing up to 40 pounds (18 kg)—the weight mostly coming from the hefty shield—the *murmillo* was categorized as heavily armed. The *murmillo's* most common foes in the arena were the similarly armored *thraex* or *hoplomachus*. The *murmillo* was known to be the

Right: A reenactor demonstrates the fighting skills of a *hoplomachus* **in the arena.**

Facing page: A nineteenth-century painting depicts a *retiarius*, **the gladiator who was often the source of ridicule among Roman spectators.**

favorite of the Emperor Domitian, who reacted particularly badly when the gladiator was criticized by a spectator in the Colosseum. Suetonius recounts the story:

> "A householder who said that a Thracian gladiator was a match for the *murmillo*, but not for the giver of the games, he caused to be dragged from his seat and thrown into the arena to dogs, with this placard: 'A favorer of the Thracians who spoke impiously.'"
> —Suetonius, *Lives of the Twelve Caesars*, translated by Thomson and Forester

Hoplomachus

The *hoplomachus* was a popular gladiator modelled on the Greek hoplite. Often confused with the *thraex*, the *hoplomachus* shared many of the same weapons and armor. Both gladiators wore padded leg wrappings, leg greaves, and a similar visored helmet. However, unlike the *thraex*, the *hoplomachus* wore quilted trousers or padded leg wrappings that began at his feet and finished just beneath his folded loincloth. The leg greaves that covered the wrappings usually reached to just above the fighter's knees. This heavy leg protection was designed to compensate for the *hoplomachus*'s small, round, convex shield. It was

usually constructed from a single sheet of bronze, and again designed to look like a smaller version of the type used by the Greek hoplite. The diminutive size of the shield enabled the *hoplomachus* to hold it along with his dagger in one hand and fight with his spear in the other, or vice versa. However, like the *thraex* and most of the other gladiators the *hoplomachus* wore no armor on his torso and instead appeared in the arena bare-chested.

The armor of a *hoplomachus* weighed up to 40 pounds (18 kg), putting him into the category of heavily-armed gladiator. He would most often be paired against similarly weighted opponents, the *murmillo* and at times the *thraex*. Although greatly popular in the western Mediterranean territories of the Roman Empire, the *hoplomachus* was less so in the east. This can perhaps be explained by the *hoplomachus*'s resemblance to the Greek hoplite, which may have been considered insulting to those states that were once part of the civilization of ancient Greece.

Retiarius

The *retiarius* fought with a net and is the most easily identifiable Roman gladiator. He was not equipped with a shield or helmet but wore a *galerus*, a metal guard, on one shoulder and carried a trident and short dagger.

The *retiarius* was not introduced to the arena until sometime after the middle of the first century CE. He did not share the warrior origins of some of his colleagues. Although clearly inspired by the sea, there is little information about how the *retiarius*

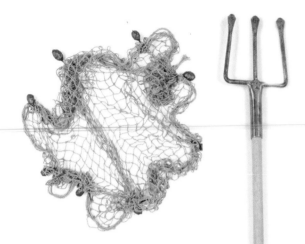

The net and trident were a *retiarius*'s main weapons. Once they had gone, the gladiator had only a dagger to fight with.

came into being. However, after being introduced to the arena he was to be a mainstay of the games up until their disappearance.

The introduction of the *retiarius* heralded a new period in the history of the games, where differently-armed fighters—instead of those more closely matched—were paired. Previously, a heavily-armed fighter like a *murmillo* would fight a similarly weighty adversary, such as a *hoplomachus*. But from the late first century, a *murmillo* might just as well meet a *retiarius* in the arena. This enabled a more unpredictable contest.

Being light and agile was a *retiarius*'s best defense against a heavily-armed opponent. He fought naked apart from a folded loincloth and on some occasions a tunic. One leg was protected by wrappings and covered by a greave. The *manica* on a *retiarius*'s arm reached up to the shoulder, which was then covered by the *galerus*. The *galerus* was made from a piece of 2.6 pounds (1.2 kg) sheet bronze that wrapped around a *retiarius*'s bicep and then angled outwards at his shoulder. This enabled a *retiarius* to bend his head behind the *galerus* and use it as a shield. *Retiarii* from eastern provinces of the Roman Empire sometimes favored a chainmail *manica* instead of a *galerus*, which also covered part of their chests.

It is an odd quirk that in the many depictions of a *retiarius* he is seldom shown wielding his net. This may have simply been because artists found it too difficult to represent. A *retiarius*'s net would have followed a standard pattern of larger mesh holes at its center to trap his opponent and smaller holes at its outer edges to snag his weapons. The smaller

holes at the edges would have given the net enough weight to stay open when it was thrown, but weights at the ends may also have been used. With a diameter of around 10 feet (3 m), a *retiarius*'s net probably weighed 4 to 6.6 pounds (2–3 kg). It was designed for throwing, and was something of a one-shot weapon for this reason. If thrown unsuccessfully a *retiarius* had to rely on his other weapons—the trident and dagger.

The trident was a *retiarius*'s main weapon, which reached to around 6 feet (1.8 m) high. The three prongs were used to stab at an opponent and also pull away his weaponry and armor. The prongs were not strong enough to pierce metal armor, but were thin enough to penetrate the eyeholes of most gladiator visors. A *retiarius*'s third weapon was the straight-bladed dagger, known as a *pugio*. This was usually a weapon of last resort, as it was never in the interest of the lightly-armed *retiarius* to be close enough to his opponent to fight with a short blade. Often the *pugio* would be used to dispatch an adversary who was already disarmed and lying defenseless on the ground.

With armor weighing a maximum of 17.6 pounds (8 kg), the *retiarius* was the most lightly-armed gladiator. He was most frequently paired with the *secutor*, the fish-like gladiator, which gave the contest the appearance of a fisherman catching fish. On some occasions, one *retiarius* would fight against two *secutores* from the position of a raised bridge, or *pons*. *Retiarii* who fought from a *pons* were known as *pontarii*, and it is likely the contest was sometimes staged

Retiarius in Combat

retiarius's fate often depended on how he fared with his net. A good first throw could bind up his opponent and end a bout within seconds. However, once thrown the net was a tricky thing to retrieve. It also left a *retiarius* without armor and only a trident and dagger to fend his adversary off. As so much hinged on his net, the *retiarius* spent a great deal of time in the *ludus* learning how to throw it. The best technique for doing so was to hold the folded net in one hand and cast it with an underarm action. This required a particular snap of the wrist so the net would take off in a circular motion and spin as it flew towards the opponent. The spinning movement ensured the net would stay open in flight and then wrap around whatever it landed against. A throw from around 6 feet 7 inches (2 m) would give the net its most confining impact, but sources also show that *retiarii* occasionally threw their net from close quarters and held on to a corner, so it could be retrieved. Once ensnared in a *retiarius*'s net, there was little an opponent could do but hope for mercy from the crowd.

Once separated from his net, the *retiarius*'s best chance of overcoming his adversary was with his main weapon, the trident. He would use it to stab at his opponent's legs, body and head, and deliver various two-handed blows. Unlike a fisherman's hooks, the prongs of the trident were not barbed and could therefore easily cut into flesh and pull out again without impediment. However, impaling his opponent

Above: Once ensnared by a *retiarius*'s net, there was little an opponent could do but hope for a *missio*.

was not the only objective—by snagging his helmet or shield, a *retiarius* without a net could put himself back into the contest on an even footing. A final use for the trident was to trip his opponent up. Once his rival was down, the *retiarius* could use his *pugio* (dagger) to finish him off or call for the sentence of the crowd.

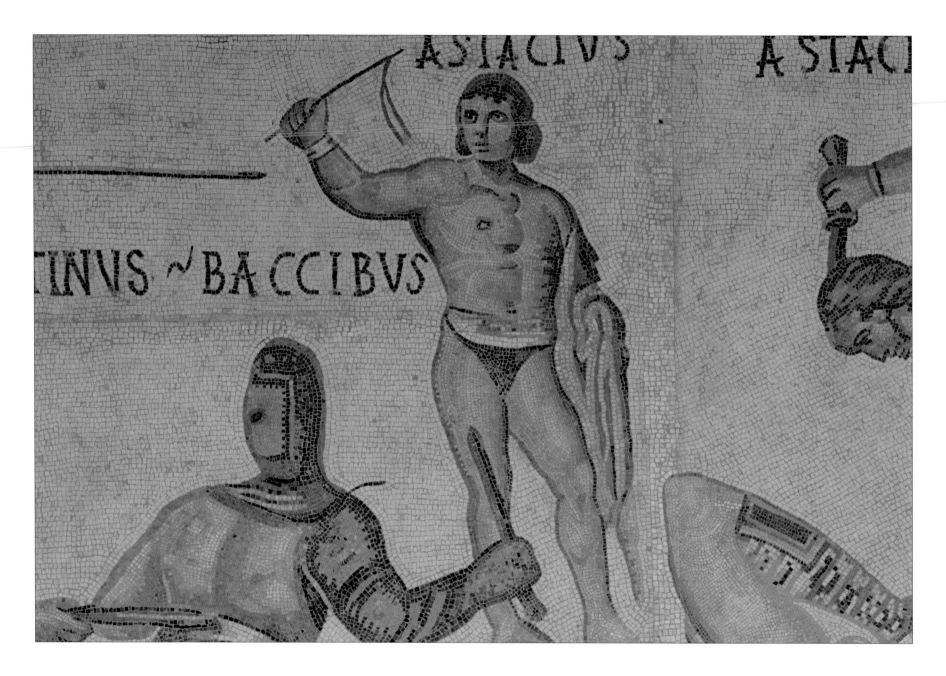

above water. The purpose of such a bout was for one of the *secutores* to mount the *pons* from the steps at either end to attack the *retiarius*. To make this outnumbering fairer, the *retiarius* was given a stack of orange-sized stone balls to throw at his opponents. It is thought that the *secutores* were forbidden from throwing the balls back at their lightly armed adversary.

Tunic-wearing Effeminates

The Roman public had something of a love-hate relationship with the *retiarius*. This was in part because the gladiator fought without armor or a helmet, which allowed the crowd to see his full identity. The *retiarius* was a favorite of Emperor Claudius, who liked to see the expressions of death on a gladiator's face. But the bareheaded gladiator was also resented by other members of the crowd. A helmet was a dehumanizing quality that many felt appropriate to the gladiator's *infamis* position. Once the helmet had been removed, spectators were not only party to the identity of the gladiator but also the facial expressions that Claudius so loved.

These humanizing aspects were often considered inappropriate for the arena, partly perhaps because they made for uncomfortable viewing. Many historians also believe that the near-nakedness of the *retiarius* meant the crowd associated them with vulnerability and effeminacy. This was even truer of a sub-group of lower-status *retiarii* who only wore tunics. These *retiarii tunicati*, who were often a source of ridicule in the arena, are alluded to by Juvenal:

"So even the *lanista*'s establishment is better ordered than yours, for he separates the vile from the decent, and sequesters even from their fellow-*retiarii* the wearers of the ill-famed tunic; in the training-school, and even in jail, such creatures herd apart."
—Juvenal, *Satire Six*, translated by G.G. Ramsay

Despite feelings of ambivalence towards the *retiarius*, the gladiator could be a popular figure in the arena. As well as providing the crowd with an easily identifiable type of gladiator that had an inherently individual fighting style, the *retiarius*'s lack of a helmet and armor often gave him sex appeal. Graffiti found in Pompeii about the *retiarius* Cresces, include: "Cresces the Netter of young girls by night." Whether adored or abhorred by the Roman public, the *retiarius* was apparently well liked enough to stay fighting in the arena until the end of the imperial age.

Secutor

The *secutor* was based on the *murmillo* and earlier *samnis*, and chiefly designed as an opponent for the *retiarius*. The only noticeable difference was the *secutor*'s helmet. This was smooth, with small eyeholes and a fin-like crest, which gave the helmet the appearance of a fish's head. Indeed, the streamlined shape of the helmet was designed to avoid being snared on the *retiarius*'s net. The eyeholes were also intended to stymie the *retiarius*'s attack, by being too small at 1 inch (3 cm) in diameter to allow the prongs of the

Facing page: Detail of a fourth-century-CE mosaic discovered in the nineteenth century at the Borghese estate near Rome.

"Once a band of five retiarii in tunics, matched against the same number of secutores, yielded without a struggle; but when their death was ordered, one of them caught up his trident and slew all the victors."

—*Suetonius*

trident through easily. The disadvantage of these small apertures was that it gave the *secutor* very limited vision and let little air into the helmet. The *secutor* often quickly became hot and breathless, so the fighter tried to avoid long contests whenever possible. The *secutor* had the added problem of carrying the large legionary's shield also used by the *murmillo*. His only weapon was the short *gladius* and it was this, combined with his limited eyesight, that made it necessary for the *secutor* to get as close to his opponent as possible.

By comparison, the lightly-armed *retiarius* would do everything he could to stay away from the *secutor*, preferring a range of around 6 feet 7 inches (2 m) from which to throw his net or strike with his trident. This often turned the contest into something of a catch and chase, until the *retiarius* had been separated from his net and trident or the *secutor* had been caught or simply run out of breath.

Commodus often fought as a *secutor* in the arena and even threatened to inaugurate the year 193 CE by appearing as one—the fatal mistake that led to his assassination. His bouts in the arena are recorded by Dio:

> "[Commodus] would fight as gladiator. The form of contest that he practiced and the armor that he used were those of the *secutores*, as they were called: he held the shield in his right hand and the wooden sword in his left, and indeed took great pride in the fact that he was left-handed."
>
> —Cassius Dio, *Roman History*, translated by Earnest Cary

Despite his early demise, Commodus made sure his legacy as a gladiator emperor lived on through the ages. After removing the head from the Colossus of Nero and replacing it with a likeness of himself, Commodus added the following inscription to the plinth below the statue:

> "Champion of *secutores*; only left-handed fighter to conquer twelve times (as I recall the number) one thousand men." Although the statue was thrown down after Commodus's death, his message has remained for posterity.

OTHER GLADIATOR TYPES

For some types of gladiators we have very little available information. Either they have been represented during the centuries of Roman history through pictorial depictions with no written information, or we have written accounts without any pictorial evidence.

Crupellarius

Mentioned by Tacitus, the *crupellarii* were so heavily armed that once down on the ground it

was impossible for them to get up again. Despite this, it seems that even in their horizontal state the *crupellarius* was virtually invulnerable. Tacitus describes legionaries trying to hack off the gladiator's armor with hachets and pickaxes as if they were "battering a wall," while the *crupellarius* was left "lying on the ground, without an effort to rise, like a dead man."

Dimachaerus

A *dimachaerus* was a gladiator who fought without a shield, but was instead armed with two swords, one of which was curved. A *dimachaerus* is pictured in a third-century-CE relief wearing short greaves and a brimmed helmet. He also has on a tunic. Some scholars believe that the *dimachaerus* only fought against gladiators of the same type.

Above: A first-century-CE bas-relief of gladiators in the arena.

Facing page: An illustration of a famous bout between the *secutor* Astyanax and the *retiarius* Kalendio.

Novelty Acts

The *andabatae* were criminals who had not been trained at a *ludus*, but were instead intended as a sort of gladiatorial comic relief. Two *andabatae* would fight armed only with a *gladius* and wearing helmets without eyeholes, which meant they were fighting blind. The gladiators would therefore stagger around the arena floor slashing and stabbing at each other until one was fortunate enough to land a killing blow. To aid the *andabatae* in their combat and help them locate each other, the crowd would shout out directions and other helpful advice. Sometimes the *andabatae* would fight from horseback, in a sadistic precursor to the medieval joust.

Fights between the *paegniarii* were another novelty act intended to warm up the crowd before the real gladiators entered. The *paegniarii* were dressed like gladiator clowns and fought each other with the wooden rudis used in gladiator training. Often the *paegniarii* were dwarves, or men with physical disabilities or missing limbs.

The men who hunted and fought against the wild animals were called *bestiarii* and *venatores*. In the imperial age, the *venatores* wore tunics or sometimes a small breastplate, and fought using spears and bow and arrows from foot or horseback. The *bestiarii* were like low-ranking *venatores* whose tasks included teasing the animals with whips and torches. The *venatores* and *bestiarii* only ever fought against the beasts in the arena and never took part in gladiatorial contests between humans.

Above: A first-century-CE bowl excavated in London showing a leopard and lion alongside a *bestiarius*.

Sagittarius

The *sagittarius* were mounted gladiators who wore plated armor, pointed helmets and fought with a bow. As this composite bow was capable of firing arrows for long distances, special security measures to protect the crowd had to be taken. *Sagittarius* would not normally fight each other, but would be pitted against a different type of gladiator.

Essedarius

Found only in literature from the imperial age and scarcely ever depicted, the *essedarius* is a hotly disputed gladiator in modern times. He was known to have fought from a light chariot and carried a small, round shield and a spear. He wore a brimless helmet adorned with two feathers, a *manica* on his sword arm and padded leg wrappings.

Facing page: A bas-relief of *thraex, hoplomachus,* and *murmillo* gladiators.

Above: A first-century-CE marble relief from a funerary monument in Pompeii showing a *pompa, venatio,* and gladiator fights.

GLADIATOR EQUIPMENT

The story of the armor and weaponry of the gladiators is of their evolution over the period between the late Republic and the fall of empire. However, much of our modern knowledge comes from the discovery of artifacts from the early imperial age. The design and materials used in the construction of these valuable finds have helped experts better understand how they were used in combat.

A treasure trove of gladiatorial armaments was unearthed during the 1766–1767 excavation of the city of Pompeii. While the unsophisticated archeological methods of the day led to the damage and loss of many items, several important artifacts survived. These included six single greaves, five pairs of greaves, three *galeri*, a round shield, and various daggers and spears. However, the greatest find of all was a collection of 15 gladiator helmets, all in pristine condition.

Helmets

The helmets found at Pompeii were so perfect and undamaged that many historians argued they could not possibly have been used in the arena. These scholars pointed to the ornate and obviously expensive embossing on the helmets as proof they were ceremonial objects only. It was suggested that the helmets were used in gladiatorial processions and replaced with plainer, hardier models for the fights themselves.

However, there are many counterarguments. The intricate decorations that adorn the helmets would have actually added an extra layer of protection. It is also unlikely that the *lanistae* and *editores* of the enormously lavish and expensive imperial games would have fretted over the cost of a few helmets. A gladiator's helmet, after all, was considered a particularly interesting and important part of his equipment. It identified the fighter and acted as an imposing showpiece for his particular category. The helmet also gave a gladiator his striking and sinister appearance—and, paradoxically, his anonymity. This prevented potential complications between dueling comrades from the same *ludus*. It also spared the crowd from difficult feelings of compassion that could arise from seeing a helmetless gladiator in pain.

The Pompeii helmets showed few signs of nicks, notches, or other damage that could be associated with an armed duel to the death. However, rather than a telltale sign that the helmets were not used in the arena, it instead raised a relevant point about the nature of gladiatorial combat. Heavy swords used for cutting and slashing at an opponent were not a feature of Roman gladiatorial equipment, nor that of its legionaries.

Instead, the short *gladius* was used to stab at an opponent's vulnerable spots and there was certainly no chance it would penetrate his armor. Gladiators, therefore, would have been unlikely to waste their energy landing blows on their adversary's helmet. However, they may well have hacked and jabbed at his visor, especially if they were armed with a spear or trident.

The most common damage to a gladiator's helmet occurred around his visor. These visors were

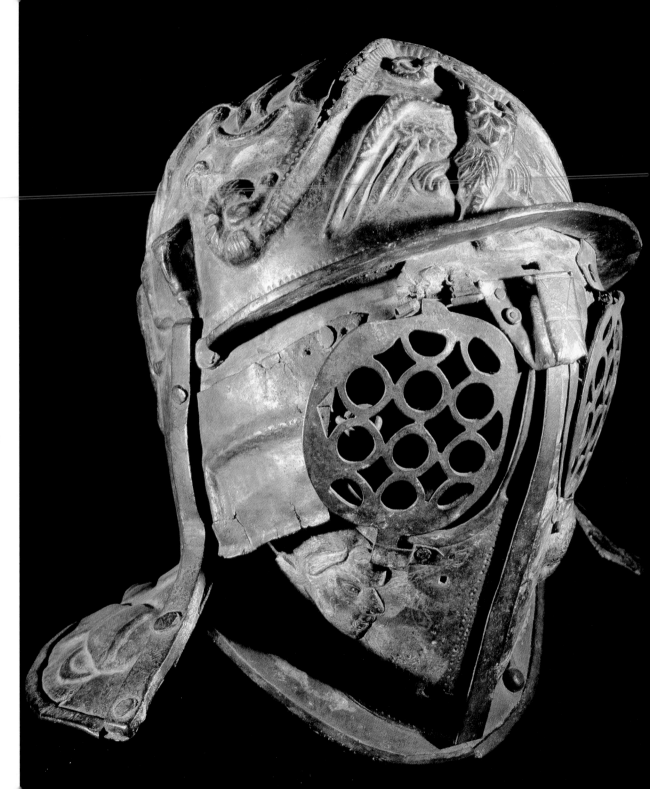

unlike those worn by medieval knights, which were raised and lowered horizontally. Instead a gladiator's visor opened in two vertical halves across his cheekbones and joined up in the middle. The two halves were then fastened with metal latches across a vertical rib, usually at points near the forehead and throat. Leather straps strengthened this arrangement. Because the visor's system of hinges, latches and fastenings were the helmet's weakest points, they were also a target for an attacker. Once a gladiator's helmet was disabled, knocked off or the visor opened, his exposed head became fair game.

The gladiator helmets found at Pompeii weighed between 6.6 to 14.4 pounds (3–7 kg), with an average weight of just under 8.8 pounds (4 kg). This is almost twice as heavy as a Roman legionary's helmet from around the same period. The extra weight reflected the gladiator's different lifestyle. A battle-ready legionary carried around 55 pounds (25 kg) of equipment, and more when he was marching. It was not practical for him to wear a heavy helmet for a long march and then potentially several hours of battle afterwards. However, a gladiator, who typically fought for an average of 10 to 15 minutes, could easily handle—and would have welcomed—the extra weight. To cushion an opponent's blow and to make the gladiator's helmet more comfortable to wear, it lay on top of layers of padding. Experts think padded quilting was either stuck onto the underside of the helmet, or a padded cap tied first to the gladiator's head. No such padding has survived into the modern age.

Manica

With their heads and necks entirely protected by a helmet, gladiators employed various other pieces of armor to cover the rest of their bodies. As most gladiators fought bare-chested—apart from *provocatores* who wore a breastplate and *equites* who wore tunics—protecting the arms was vitally important. This was the job of the *manica*, a thick, padded arm guard made from layers of cloth, leather and, in the later years of the empire, metal.

Initially, a *manica* was only designed to protect the hand and arm up to the elbow and was based on the boxing glove, or *caestus*. It was fastened to the hand by leather loops across the thumb and fingers and attached to the arm with leather straps. This short *manica* weighed around 2.2 pounds (1 kg) and was designed to enable the full range of movement in the arm. While guarding the arm against sword cuts, the *manica* also protected the wearer from the inevitable bumps and bruises caused by hitting his own shield.

The arm carrying the shield, however, did not suffer from the same problem and was not normally equipped with a *manica*. Longer *manicae* that reached up to the shoulder were later developed for gladiators such as the *retiarius*, and towards the end of the imperial age metal scale armor and chainmail sometimes took the place of the traditional *manica* materials.

The purpose of protecting a gladiator's arms was to prevent any sword cuts, intentional or accidental, that could disable the fighter and end a bout too quickly. By slicing the large tendons

Facing page: **A bronze *provocator* helmet from the excavated gladiatorial school in Pompeii.**

"Champion of secutores; only left-handed fighter to conquer twelve times (as I recall the number) one thousand men."

—*Inscription on Commodus's statue*

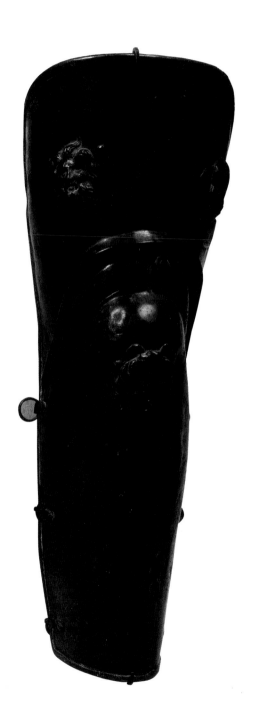

Facing page: A third-century-CE mosaic of a *thraex* armed with a *sica*, a curved sword.

Left: Bronze greaves shielded the shins and sometimes rose above the knees. Gladiators would attach leg wrappings known as *fasciae* underneath for added protection.

around a fighter's elbow or behind his knee, a gladiator could render his opponent's limbs useless. For this reason, similar wrapping to the *manicae* that protected the arms was also used on the legs underneath a gladiator's greaves.

Greaves

Gladiator greaves, or shin guards, were based on those of the archaic Greek hoplite. Unlike the hoplite, whose greaves wrapped around the whole lower leg, the Roman greave only protected the leg's front and part of its sides. Greaves were made from a single sheet of bronze and adorned with embossing.

The size of a gladiator's greaves was normally determined by the length of his shield. Those carrying a large, rectangular shield, such as the *murmillo* and *secutor*, used only knee-high greaves, while small-shield carriers such as the *thraex* and *hoplomachus* wore greaves above the knee. Sometimes this principle was ignored. The *dimachaerus*, for example, fought without a shield but only wore greaves below the knee. This must have made his legs an easy target for an opponent. It is equally surprising that the *equites*, who wore wrapping on their legs, did not further protect themselves with greaves. Leg

Right: Reenactors play the parts of a *hoplomachus* and *thraex* on an arena floor.

wrappings were known as *fasciae* and made of the same quilted cloth as *manicae*. The wrappings were worn at varying heights on a gladiator's legs and could reach up to his loincloth.

The loincloth, or *subligaculum*, was a piece of heavy, folded cloth that hung like an inverted triangle from the waist. The loincloth was held in place by the *balteus*, a broad leather belt, around 3.5 inches (9 cm) wide and covered in bronze.

Shields

The large, rectangular-shaped shield favored by the *murmillo* and *secutor* was based on the *scutum* shield used by the Roman legionaries. As this *scutum* evolved over the ages, so did the gladiator's. During the Republic the shield was oval in shape, but by the mid-first century CE it had become rectangular with sharp edges.

The slightly curved shield was constructed from three layers of wooden sheets and measured between 39 to 47 inches (100–120 cm) in height and 23 to 31 inches (60–80 cm) wide. An extra wooden strip ran vertically down the middle of the shield and an outward-facing bronze dome fitted to its center. The shield was protected by a layer of felt or leather and reinforced with bronze or iron edges. Embossed or painted decorations adorned the front, and in total the shield weighed around 17.6 pounds (8 kg).

The smaller shields used by the *hoplomachus* and *thraex* weighed around 4.4 pounds (2 kg) and 6.6 pounds (3 kg) respectively. An example of an *hoplomachus*'s round shield from the Pompeii excavations was made from one piece of bronze

and measured 14.5 inches (37 cm) in diameter. The square shield of the *thraex*, by comparison, was around 19.6 by 23.6 inches (50 by 60 cm), and constructed in the same way as the *scutum*. Another small round shield was that used by the *equites*, roughly 19.6 inches (50 cm) in diameter and made from compressed leather.

These small shields had a duel purpose: they were employed as both defensive and offensive weapons. Firstly a gladiator would use his shield to parry blows and then punch and swing it in a counterattack. A metal dome on a small shield could be used as a knuckleduster, easily breaking bone or putting large dents into an opponent's helmet and armor.

Weapons

The first gladiators were depicted using spears as their primary weapon, although by the imperial age spears were favored only by the *equites*, *hoplomachi*, and *essedarii*. Around 6.5 feet (2 m) long, these spears originally had a bronze spearhead with a broadleaf shape.

From the late Republic, the gladiator's main weapon was the *gladius* sword. To start with, the *gladius* had a double-edged steel blade around 25.5 inches (65 cm) long and 1.9 inches (5 cm) wide, but in the first century BCE it was shortened to 19.6 inches (50 cm) long and 3.1 inches (8 cm) wide. In the first century CE, the dimensions of the *gladius* changed again, with a 17.7-inch-long (45 cm) blade that was 2.3 inches (6 cm) wide. The hilt of a *gladius* was usually constructed from ivory with a wooden pommel.

Above: The bronze shield of a *hoplomachus* gladiator discovered at Pompeii.

The gladiator swords found at Pompeii had blades measuring between 11.8 inches (30 cm) and 15.7 inches (40 cm) long, and were probably used by the *retiarii* and *hoplomachi*. The curved *sica* sword used by the *thraex*, by comparison, could feature a blade as long as 23.6 inches (60 cm) with a curvature of 45 degrees. By the third century CE the legionary's *gladius* had been largely replaced by the longer *spatha* sword. With a blade measuring 27.5 inches (70 cm) long by 3.34 inches (8.5 cm) wide, the *spatha* was often also favored by gladiators during the late imperial age.

THE SETTING

Gladiator fights were designed to be public spectacles from the time the first *munera* were staged in the early Roman Republic. As the events grew larger and more extravagant, purpose-built arenas were constructed. The first of these arenas was in Campania, the birthplace of the gladiators. Today, the oldest surviving arena is an amphitheater in Pompeii, dating from around 70 BCE. This Pompeian model was based on the first amphitheaters built in Rome during the first century BCE. Before these arenas, *munera* in Rome were presented in the city's Forum Borium and Forum Romanum. Here, makeshift seating was put up for the ever-increasing numbers of spectators.

The new wooden amphitheaters of the first century BCE were built specifically for gladiatorial contests and provided permanent seating. One of the first arenas was designed by the aristocrat Gaius Scribonius Curio, who constructed an amphitheater of two rotating, semicircular halves. This enabled separate theatrical performances to be held in each half before they were swivelled around and joined up to make the amphitheater. There are no surviving remains of Curio's innovation today, which was certainly constructed by the politician to curry favor with the Senate. In particular, Curio was a great supporter of Caesar, and according to Tacitus he was on the dictator's payroll. He also died fighting for Caesar during the bloody civil war with Pompey.

It was Caesar who built Rome's second wooden amphitheater in 46 BCE. This provided seating around a central elliptical-shaped arena, where the largest and most lavish games yet staged in Rome took place. Rome's first stone amphitheater was

Below: A *gladius* sword dating from the first century CE.

built in 29 BCE by Titus Statilius Taurus, and several others followed in the imperial age. Augustus, Caligula and Nero all built amphitheaters to hold their games, but none could top the greatest arena of them all: the Colosseum.

Completed in 80 CE, the Colosseum served as the blueprint for every other amphitheater that sprung up around the colonies of the Roman Empire during the heyday of arena building in the second century CE. These included notable arenas in Lyon, France, and Merida in Spain. It was in the interests of foreign Roman towns and cities to prove their dedication to the imperial cult through the building of impressive arenas and many spared no expense doing so. In Arles, France, a large stone amphitheater was constructed with an arena floor measuring 228 by 125 feet (69 by 38 m) and seating for 23,000 spectators. In 232 CE, a particularly impressive amphitheater with seating for 40,000 people was built in El Djem in present-

Above: The Colosseum in Rome as it stands today. The arena floor has long since gone, revealing the _hypogeum_ below.

Facing page: The third-century-CE amphitheater built in the ancient city of Thysdrus, modern day El Djem, Tunisia, was the most impressive Roman structure in North Africa.

Bloodshed at Pompeii

While there are few recorded incidents of unruly crowds at Roman amphitheaters, an exception occurred in Pompeii in 59 BCE. The events are described by Tacitus:

"About the same time a trifling beginning led to frightful bloodshed between the inhabitants of Nuceria and Pompeii, at a gladiatorial show exhibited by Livineius Regulus, who had been, as I have related, expelled from the Senate. With the unruly spirit of townsfolk, they began with abusive language of each other; then they took up stones and at last weapons, the advantage resting with the populace of Pompeii, where the show was being exhibited. And so there were brought to Rome a number of the people of Nuceria, with their bodies mutilated by wounds, and many lamented the deaths of children or of parents. The emperor entrusted the trial of the case to the Senate, and the Senate to the consuls, and then again the matter being referred back to the senators, the inhabitants of Pompeii were forbidden to have any such public gathering for ten years, and all associations they had formed in defiance of the laws were dissolved. Livineius and the others who had excited the disturbance were punished with exile."

—Tacitus, *The Annals*, Translated by Alfred Church and William Brodribb

Above: A fresco from 59 CE depicting the violent brawl between the people of Nuceria and Pompeii.

day Tunisia. To date, the remains of 186 arenas have been discovered in what was the Roman Empire, but more were certainly built.

The largest Roman amphitheaters had a floor area of 197 to 262 by 98 by 164 feet (60–80 by 30–50 m). This space was needed not so much for the gladiator fights themselves but the various *venationes* and processions that preceded the afternoon contests. The floors of the arenas were covered with sand, which usually lay across a wooden floor. Underneath the arena floor was a complex of corridors and chambers known as a *hypogeum*.

The *hypogeum* was like a giant backstage where props, animals, gladiators, and people to be executed were kept underground before making their entrance. A system of ropes, pulleys, and lifts would bring man and beast from the *hypogeum* through trapdoors into the arena. This meant, for example, a man bound to a frame could appear as if by magic in the center of the arena. Then animals would emerge from trapdoors dotted around, ready to make their attack. This system also allowed whole sets of trees and bushes to be suddenly brought up to the top for the *venatio*, or the dramatically staged mythological stories used in the execution of slaves and criminals.

Some amphitheaters, including the one in Verona, Italy, were constructed to hold a basin of water underneath the arena floor. The floor was then uncovered in the staging of special aquatic events such as the hunting of crocodiles or hippopotamuses. Mythological stories would also be reenacted on this watery stage, as were mini-*naumachaie* using small boats and miniature ships.

Precautions were needed to shield the spectators from the men and beasts in the arena. Most amphitheaters had a permanent 13-foot (4 m) high podium wall that separated the crowd from the arena floor. This barrier was often extended with high nets for specific performances. Big cats, in particular, were known to jump higher than the wall when their lives were at stake. After the revolt of Spartacus, particular care was also taken to stop a breakout of gladiators occurring at an amphitheater. Gladiators and those doomed to execution were kept under careful supervision before they entered the arena and a large contingent of legionaries stationed around the amphitheater added a further layer of protection. Interestingly, there were more reported incidents of violence at Roman circuses and theaters than at its arenas. This often had to do with clashes between fans of opposing chariot teams and the occasional riot over the content of a stage play.

Amphitheaters were not the only venues for gladiator contests during the imperial period. In Gaul, spectacles were held in semi-circular buildings that more closely resembled theaters than arenas. In the provinces east of Rome, gladiatorial games were almost always held in ordinary stage theaters. In Athens, the Theater of Dionysus situated just below the Acropolis was the main setting for the gladiator fights. Where necessary, these venues were fitted with wooden walls and nets to protect the public from wild animals and rogue gladiators.

In the frontier towns of the empire's far reaches, amphitheaters were often built near the forts of the Roman garrison. These arenas were used for meetings, parades and drills as well as gladiatorial contests. The games were designed to entertain the legionaries and provide a piece of Rome away from Rome while also reminding them of the important virtues of bravery and a contempt for death they might soon need in real life.

There is little doubt, however, that the legionaries charged with keeping Rome's frontiers trouble free would have gladly given up their provincial seat for one inside the greatest amphitheater of the ancient world—Rome's Colosseum.

The Colosseum
The 64 CE fire of Rome had cleared a large space in the center of the city for rebuilding—both literally and symbolically. Nero's destructive reign had left Rome battered and singed and in 70 CE Emperor Vespasian began the construction of the *Amphitheatrum Flavium*. The chosen site for the amphitheater was where a lake sat on the grounds of Nero's hated Golden House. The building of the amphitheater was designed as a restorative gesture that would usher in a period of rebirth for the city. Ironically the Colosseum took its common name from the bronze statue of Nero—the *Colossus Neronis*—that had stood close by.

To build the Colosseum, tens of thousands of slaves and prisoners of war captured in the Jerusalem uprising drained the lake and excavated more than 30,000 tons of earth. Solid rock foundations were then laid 13 to 39 feet (4–12 m) deep. Over 100,000 tons of travertine rock was

"With the unruly spirit of townsfolk, they began with abusive language of each other; then they took up stones and at last weapons."

—*Tacitus*

imported to build the structure of the amphitheater on a series of columns and arches, and 300 tons of iron were used to clamp it all together. Thousands of tons of marble then lined the building's facade and were used to carve the dozens of statues that adorned the upper arches of its 164 feet (50 m) high outer wall.

> *"Titus suddenly filled this same theater with water and brought in horses and bulls and some other domesticated animals."*
>
> —*Cassius Dio*

When it was completed, the Colosseum was a marvel of archways, steps, seating, and Doric and Corinthian columns, built around seven concentric rings that encircled the central elliptical arena. The sandy arena measured 262 by 148 feet (80 by 45 m) and was surrounded by a 13-foot (4 m) high wall, above which rose several tiers of seating. According to contemporary sources, there was enough seating for around 87,000 people, but modern estimates put it between 50,000 and 70,000.

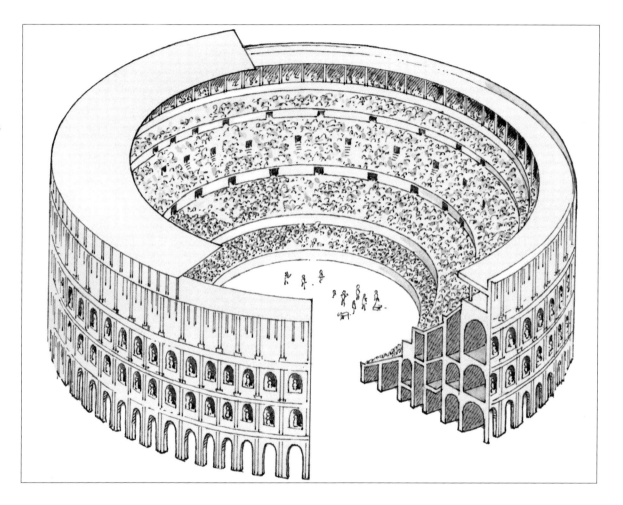

The Colosseum's seating was divided along lines of class and rank. Closest to the arena was the emperor's box, which sat on the long side of the arena, with the *editor*'s box situated on the opposite side. Next to these boxes was seating for the Vestal Virgins—the only women who were allowed so close to the action—and the senators, most of who

Above: A cutaway of the Colosseum. The blue strip around the top shows where the awning was placed to shade the audience below.

Facing page: The Theater of Dionysus in Athens was often used for gladiatorial contests during the Roman period.

had a regular seats fitted with permanent name plaques. Above them sat the knights and visiting dignitaries, followed by Roman aristocrats and citizens. The following tier was for poorer Roman citizens, as well as slaves and foreigners. The final rows at the top of the Colosseum were reserved for women—the wives, daughters, and mothers of Roman senators and nobles.

The curious arrangement for women spectators is best explained by the unbridled lust for a gladiator that could apparently strike a Roman woman of rank without warning. The oft-given contemporary example was of Eppia, the senator's wife who left her comfortable life in Rome to pursue a traveling gladiator in Egypt. It was unlikely that the Vestal Virgins would be similarly enflamed, however, as they had sworn a vow of chastity. The punishment for breaking this vow made such an action improbable—the offending Virgin would be locked away in an underground chamber with only enough food and water to last a few days.

Like all amphitheaters, the floor of the Colosseum was laid with a thick layer of sand that covered the *hypogeum* below. Before the *hypogeum* was built (during Domitian's reign) Titus held a *naumachia* at the Colosseum. Cassius Dio recounts the event:

"Titus suddenly filled this same theater with water and brought in horses and bulls and some other domesticated animals that had been taught to behave in the liquid element just as on land. He also brought in people on ships, who engaged in a sea-fight there, impersonating the Corcyreans and Corinthians."
—Cassius Dio, *Roman History*, translated by Earnest Cary

The flooding of the arena would have helped clean away the blood and viscera left behind after the violence. After the *hypogeum* was constructed, the smell was known to have become almost unbearable on hot days. To counter the stench, jets of perfumed water were pumped up from tanks in the *hypogeum* and sprayed over the crowd through a sprinkler system.

The sun was kept off those in the higher tiers with an awning system of large sails that were suspended on large poles. Roman sailors were specially employed to put together the rigging and hoist out the awning. This cover did not reach the seats nearest to the arena, but the senators occupying these seats stayed cool under large parasols.

On one occasion, the spectators were denied their protective cover and made to sit in the searing heat by the very man charged with organizing their comfort—Caligula. This would have been harsh medicine for a crowd that had been sitting in the sun for several days running. For once the spectators felt a whiff of the agony of the arena.

A Day at the Games

The imperial games followed a set sequence of events that had been tried, tested, and perfected over the centuries of Roman *munera*. The daylong bill of butchery and bloodshed began with the animal events in the morning. Lunchtime was reserved for the public execution of criminals and enemies of the state. The main attraction, however, was saved for the afternoon: the gladiator fights.

The games held at large amphitheaters such as the Colosseum of Rome ran for days and sometimes weeks. They required extraordinary organization and forward planning. Like the spectacle itself, this preparation followed an established formula.

To start, the *editor* holding the games would meet with the *lanista* to agree on the numbers and types of gladiators that would be supplied. The *editor* would then advertise the event to the public. Criers would read out the details of the spectacle in the forum, at the Circus, or at theatrical performances. Written advertisements called *edicta muneris* were displayed on city walls,

Facing page: This illustration expresses a nineteenth-century view of a morning *venatio* in the amphitheater at Pompeii.

Right: This bas-relief shows a *retiarius* who called himself Apollonius.

gates and other public spaces. The *edicta* were usually carefully designed and composed in red paint by professional poster artists. Each poster announced the occasion or person being honored by the games (often the emperor), the name of the *editor*, number of gladiator pairs performing and the name of their *gladiatorial familia*. Following this would be details of the other entertainments being provided (such as *venatio*, athletic contests, and executions), measures provided for the crowd's comfort (such as sun awnings or the spraying of perfumed water) and finally the place, time and duration of the spectacle. Dozens of *edicta muneris* have survived on the walls of Pompeii, including the following example from around 50 CE:

"Twenty pairs of gladiators belonging to Decimus Lucretius Satrius Valens, perpetual priest of Nero Caesar, son of Augustus, and twenty pairs of gladiators belonging to Decimus Lucretius Valens, his son, will fight at Pompeii

on the sixth, fifth, fourth, third, and second days before the Ides of April."
—Pompeian *Edicta Muneris* CIL IV.3884

A day or two before the spectacle began, the gladiators were paraded in a public place such as the forum. This would be followed by a banquet, called a *cena libera*, on the evening before the games began. This was another way of introducing the gladiators to the spectators who would watch them fight the next day. It was also considered the right of every gladiator, *venator,* and condemned criminal to a final feast before their day of reckoning in the arena. Smart gladiators did not gorge themselves on the rich and exotic food that was such a contrast to their daily gruel. As they knew, this often led to unneeded bowel problems before the fight. Instead, the veterans used the occasion to say goodbye to their loved ones and make any last arrangements.

Right: The *Edicta Muneris CIL 4.1189* advertised a gladiatorial spectacle in Pompeii.

Facing page: A seventeenth-century painting of gladiators about to parade themselves before the crowd without their armor, as part of a *pompa*.

It was at the *cena libera* that the *libellus munerarius*, a more detailed program of the next day's events, was made available. This would list the gladiator pairs and the order of their appearance. Each gladiator normally took a stage name, such as "Hermes, the god of the underworld"; or "Flamma, the flame." The *libellus munerarius* also listed the gladiator's number of fights and his victories to date. The *compositio*, or pairing of the gladiators, was arranged by the *editor* with the help of the *lanista* and his *ludus doctores*. The *compositio* was an important task designed to pit together two gladiators of similar ability and experience, so the contest would provide interesting sport that did not end too quickly. However, there are examples of a novice gladiator being paired up with a veteran.

A famous example about the novice fighter Marcus Attilius was recorded in an inscription. Attilius was a free man fighting as a *murmillo*, who defeated the *thraex* Hilarus in his first bout in the arena. This was no mean feat—Hilarus was a seasoned combatant who had 13 victories under his belt. Attilius went on to beat another veteran in

"The gladiator family of Aulus Suettius Cerius the aedile will fight at Pompeii on the last day of May. There will be a venatio *and awnings."*

—*Edicta Muneris CIL 4.1189*

Above: One of the second-century-CE mosaics discovered in a seaside Roman villa near Zliten, Libya, depicting various gladiatorial contests.

Facing page: The third-century-CE *Magerius Mosiac*, from a villa near El Djem, Tunisia. It features the organizer, Magerius, with huntsmen provided by theatrical producers the Telegenii.

his next appearance, a *thraex* called Lucius Raecius Felix, who similarly had won the victor's wreath 12 times. It is notable that both Hilarus and Raecius were granted a *missio* (reprieve) after fighting against Attilius and allowed to walk free.

Inscriptions and graffiti provide important clues about Roman spectacles—written descriptions of a day at the games are scarce. Contemporary authors such as Martial wrote some accounts of the arena, although these tend to be fragmented and often concentrate more on the *venationes* than the gladiator fights.

Instead, much of what we know about the contests comes from the frescos and mosaics left behind in Roman houses. Notably, the Zliten mosaic in Libya and various reliefs and frescos found in Pompeii have provided a wealth of

information. Located near the ancient Roman town of Leptis Magna, the Zliten mosaic depicts an entire spectacle from start to end. It includes the gladiatorial fights, the midday executions and of course the animal fights and hunts that began the day's entertainment.

ANIMALS OF THE ARENA

A day at the games began in much the same way as a major sporting event today, with throngs of people heading towards the arena. These spectators entered the amphitheater in their thousands and, armed with snacks, cushions for comfort, and plenty of gossip about the day's events, made their way to their seats. In the Colosseum this meant navigating steep staircases and covered walkways before emerging in the open air of the arena itself. The social structure of Roman society was mirrored in the amphitheater—the white togas of the patricians covered the lower quarters of the seating and above them the multicolored tunics of the plebeians.

The chatter from the morning crowd would intermingle with the more sinister sounds coming from the *hypogeum* beneath them. Trumpeting elephants, growling lions, and howling wolves made their desperation audible as they paced in their tiny cages. The sounds would act as a great livener for the crowd who had taken their seats and were watching the aristocracy arrive below them.

Romans loved the animal events, which had first been staged during the Republic's Punic Wars with Carthage. This was when Rome conquered foreign

Right: A *venator* spears a leopard in this mosaic.

territories with exotic animals such as elephants that could be paraded during triumphs in the capital. Because of the large numbers exported for these processions and the subsequent boredom at simply watching them walk around, the first *venationes* were staged in the Circus Maximus. Early *venatores* (animal hunters) and the more lowly *bestiarii* (animal fighters) were recruited from the same ranks as gladiators—prisoners of war, criminals, slaves, and volunteers. To start with these animal hunters and fighters wore the same armaments as the gladiators: greaves, helmets, loincloths, and swords. These later gave way to the simple tunics, leg wrappings, and spears of the late Republic and early imperial age.

Competition between Republican aristocrats and generals required that increasing numbers of animals be brought to Rome and killed for the public's amusement. Pompey's games saw the slaughter of 600 lions, 410 leopards, 20 elephants, and the first rhinoceros brought to the capital. Augustus boasts of killing 3,500 animals during his various spectacles. But this was a trifle compared to the games held by his imperial successors; at the inauguration of the Colosseum, Titus had over 9,000 beasts slaughtered. In 107 CE, Emperor Trajan went one step further by putting to death 11,000 animals during the games celebrating his victories over Dacia.

As the imperial age wore on, and the numbers of exotic animals decreased, Roman emperors chose to compete with their predecessors by providing

new and novel ways of slaughtering animals rather than just increasing their numbers. This led to great variations within the three-part morning schedule. This typically started with the animal fights, followed by circus acts and finished with the animal hunts—the great climax that symbolized the emperor's victory over nature.

As the morning events got underway in the amphitheater, the first animals were often brought up into the arena through trapdoors in the sandy floor. Neither the animals nor the spectators knew till the moment of release which beasts would fight. The crowd's favorite combats were always extreme or unusual pairings. The Zliten mosaic

Animal Catching

Catching new and unusual animals from the furthest reaches of Rome's borders often fell to the legionaries stationed there. These soldiers could become expert hunters of particular beasts and were exempt from their everyday duties to go hunting. The simplest method was to place a cage at the bottom of a pit and cover the hole with branches, leaves and a piece of bait. Once the animal had taken the bait and fallen into the pit, its cage was simply lifted out. Or the animal was coaxed to a cage by some live bait tied up in front of it. One the animal had taken the bait, hunters on horseback closed in from all sides and chased their prey into the cage. The third method was for mounted hunters shouting and waving flaming torches to chase their quarry into a netted enclosure. More obscure

Above: A fresco of a *venatio* shows two *bestiarii* behind shields trying to catch an attacking lion's attention.

and unreliable methods of capture included luring a tiger into a cage by placing a mirror inside it. Once the tiger had ventured in—supposedly to help its young that it thought was reflected back at it—the big cat found itself imprisoned.

Those animals unlucky enough to be caught then suffered the long journey back to Rome aboard carts and ships. It usually took months for these animals to reach Rome and thousands did not survive the trip. Many died from illness and malnourishment, while other fell victim to shipwrecks. There were instances, too, of animals breaking free from their cages. Some recorded examples even occurred on the streets of Rome, and a law was passed that provided compensation to the family of a citizen killed by an errant animal.

showed one case of a bear against a bull. The animals are depicted chained together, with a naked man in the middle pulling them apart with a hook. Other popular combinations included a leopard fighting a lion, a bull against an elephant, and a buffalo with a rhinoceros. Martial describes one particular battle between a tiger and a lion:

> "A tigress that had been accustomed to lick the hand of her unsuspecting keeper, an animal of rare beauty from the Hyrcanian mountains, became enraged and lacerated with maddened tooth against a fierce lion; a strange occurrence, such as had never been known in any age. She attempted nothing of the sort while she lived in the depth of the forests; but since she has been amongst us, she has acquired greater ferocity."
> —Martial, *Epigrams*, translated by R. Pears

Above: A man pulls apart a bear and a bull on the Zliten mosaic, Libya.

Facing page: A fourth-century-CE mosaic from the Villa Romana del Casale in Sicily shows the capture of wild animals bound for the Colosseum.

While searching for unpredictable combinations, many *editores* found that the animals brought from distant countries were similarly unpredictable when let loose in the amphitheater. After traveling hundreds of miles across land and sea, these animals had often been starved and locked up under the arena for days on end. Some, confronted with

thousands of shouting faces, simply slunk back into the furthest corners of their cages. However, these reluctant participants were eventually forced out by attendants with torches of burning straw or smoldering iron bars.

Other animals, maddened and angry, attacked anything they encountered. Romans loved the rhinoceroses because they were unpredictable, but also usually grumpy and aggressive. Martial recounts one episode where a rhino gained its second wind after seemingly giving up the fight:

> "At length the fury we once knew returned. For
> with his double horn he tossed a heavy bear as
> a bull tosses dummies from his head to the stars
> … He lifted two steers with his mobile neck, to
> him yielded the fierce buffalo and the bison. A
> panther fleeing before him ran headlong upon
> the spears."

—Martial, *De Spectaculis*, translated by T.R. Glover

After the animal fights had run their course, the *editor* provided some light relief. This included animal athletics and circus acts, such as elephants dancing and walking on tight ropes. A mock hunt by trained predators that included tigers, leopards, and bears would follow, with the beasts chasing down smaller animals such as rabbits and delivering them unharmed into their master's hands.

As the animals and trainers involved in the circus acts left the arena, the *venatores* rode in. This was the climax of the morning's events and a favorite with the crowd. It was also when the complex systems of the *hypogeum* were put to effective use. First, a set of trees and bushes would emerge from below the arena, popping up through trapdoors in the floor. Then flocks of harmless herbivores such as ostriches, deer, and gazelles would be let loose to run frantically through this makeshift forest. This began the chase, as mounted *venatores* hunted down the animals and slaughtered them with spears and bows and arrows.

> "*With his double horn he tossed a heavy bear as a bull tosses dummies from his head to the stars.*"
>
> —*Martial*

Soon the sandy amphitheater floor would be littered with corpses and soaked with blood. There was a pause as arena hands dragged away the dead animals with long hooks and added fresh sand. Even at this early stage in the day's program, there would be a rank smell of blood and viscera. To help make the spectators more comfortable, perfumed water was sprayed from jets out over the seats. Once the arena was cleared of debris, the large and savage animals, such as lions, panthers, and bears, were released from their cages. More *venatores* would hunt them down with spears, swords, and on occasion their bare hands. One particularly

Above: A late nineteenth-century French engraving of a gladiatorial *venatio*.

dangerous example was a type of rodeo featuring bulls. Here, bullfighters called *taurocentae* would jump from their horses on to the bulls' backs, wrestle them to the ground and strangle them.

Those *venatores* who fought on foot clearly ran a greater risk of injury or death than their mounted counterparts. Although arming the *venatores*

in the nature of gladiators went out of fashion during the Republican age, *venatores* mounted or on foot still carried a long spear. This must have given them something of an advantage, as the event was supposed to show Rome's domination over its foreign animals and winning the bouts was important. However, the *missio*, or reprieve, used during the gladiator fights also applied to the *venatio*. A *venator* who had been overcome with injury or exhaustion could appeal to the crowd for mercy. If successful his animal adversary would be taken away and he could leave the arena with his life. But if the *missio* was turned down, the *venator* simply had to go on fighting. Just to prove the odds were not always stacked on the side of man, beasts were also sometimes granted a *missio*. In the same way a veteran gladiator was rewarded for his number of victories, a famous lion or bear that had dispatched several *venatores* was sometimes allowed to live to fight another day.

While *venatores* did not receive the same acclaim and respect as the gladiators, some were able to win over the crowd and achieve fame. One such performer was Carpophorus, who Martial compares to the mythical heroes Hercules and Meleager:

> "That which was the utmost glory of Meleager, a boar put to flight—was that it? A mere portion of that of Carpophorus. He, in addition, planted his hunting-spear in a fierce rushing bear, the monarch in the realm of the northern pole; he also laid low a lion remarkable for its unheard-of sire—a lion, which might have become the hands of Hercules; and he then, with a wound from a distance, stretched lifeless a fleet leopard. And when at length he carried off his prizes, he was still in a condition to engage in new combats."

—Martial, *Epigrams*, translated by R. Pearse

Towards the end of the morning the crowd was often restless and ready for a break. It was the job of the *editor* to ensure those spectators that left the amphitheater at lunchtime would feel exhilarated and satisfied by the morning's entertainment. Many things, of course, could leave a crowd deflated and disappointed. The spectators enjoyed the sport of the hunt, even when the odds were heavily stacked against the animals, but they were less keen on slaughter just for the sake of it. An example recorded by Martial conveys the failure of a *venatio* when the audience's sympathies come into play. The event he describes features a hunt with wild pigs, one of which turns out to be heavily pregnant:

> "A light spear having pierced a pregnant she-boar, one of her litter leaped forth from the wound of its wretched mother … was this

---

The Emperor's Hunts

As the *venatio* symbolized the emperor's victory over nature, the hunts were often greatly enjoyed by the Roman rulers. Commodus used to enter the arena to hunt personally, or otherwise fling spears from the emperor's box. There were few limits for an emperor dreaming up memorable variations on the *venatio*. In 203 CE, Septimus Severus marked his tenth year as emperor with an altogether original hunt. For this event, a boat with 400 wild animals inside was placed in the arena and then designed to fall apart as if shipwrecked. The animals pouring out of the holes in the boat, which included panthers, lions, ostriches, bears, and donkeys, were then hunted down by the *venatores* riding into the arena. The hunting and killing of these animals was met with great applause.

On another occasion, Emperor Probus's attempt to invent a new *venatio* for his 281 CE triumph fell flat. After dressing the arena to look like a forest, thousands of herbivores were released and killed. This was later followed by hundreds of lions and bears. But the audience was apparently unimpressed by the animals reportedly unwilling to provide them with the sport they wanted:

> "All of these were slaughtered as they came out of the doors of their dens, and being killed in this way they afforded no great spectacle. For there was none of that rush on the part of the beasts which takes place when they are let loose from cages. Besides, many, unwilling to charge, were dispatched with arrows. Then he brought out one hundred leopards from Libya, then one hundred from Syria, then one hundred lionesses and at the same time three hundred bears; all of which beasts, it is clear, made a spectacle more vast than enjoyable."

—Flavius Vopiscus of Syracuse, *Historia Augusta: Life of Probus*, translated by David Magie

a delivery? She would willingly have died wounded by more weapons, that this sad way to life might have been opened to all her young ones … nor did the litter lie still-born, but ran about while its mother was falling. Oh! how great invention is evoked by sudden chances!"
—Martial, *Epigrams*, translated by Walter C.A. Ker

This bizarre incident must have made many such as Martial reflect on the issues of life and death as they left the amphitheater. After several hours of animal slaughter, the morning events were now over.

LUNCHTIME EXECUTIONS

The public executions at lunchtime were a great crowd divider, both literally and metaphorically. Many spectators used the period to leave the amphitheater and relieve themselves in the public toilets outside or take a bite to eat in one of the nearby bars. Others left for moralistic reasons. Many patricians, in particular, accepted the executions as necessary, but did not want to stay to watch. For them, the executions were a bloodshed too far, a pointless spectacle performed without honor. Writer Seneca describes this moral viewpoint:

"The men have no defensive armor. They are exposed to blows at all points, and no one ever strikes in vain. Many persons prefer this program to the usual pairs and to the bouts "by request." Of course they do; there is no helmet or shield to deflect the weapon. What is the need of defensive armor, or of skill?

Left: This second-century-CE fresco shows a lightly-armed *venator* taking on a lion.

Facing page: An illustration of a Christian martyr being manhandled before the emperor.

Below: Martial was a first-century-CE Roman poet born in Spain who painted a wry view of Roman society in his epigrams.

All these mean delaying death. In the morning they throw men to the lions and the bears; at noon, they throw them to the spectators. The spectators demand that the slayer shall face the man who is to slay him in his turn; and they always reserve the latest conqueror for another butchering. The outcome of every fight is death, and the means are fire and sword. This sort of thing goes on while the arena is empty. You may retort: 'But he was a highway robber; he killed a man!' And what of it? Granted that, as a murderer, he deserved this punishment, what crime have you committed, poor fellow, that you should deserve to sit and see this show? In the morning they cried 'Kill him! Lash him! Burn him! Why does he meet the sword in so cowardly a way? Why does he strike so feebly? Why doesn't he die game? Whip him to meet his wounds! Let them receive blow for blow, with chests bare and exposed to the stroke!' And when the games stop for the intermission, they announce: 'A little throat-cutting in the meantime, so that there may still be something going on!'"
—Seneca, *Moral Letters to Lucilius*, translated by Richard M. Gummere

Martial disagreed. His counterargument justified the lunchtime executions as maintaining the natural order. Any who opposed the might of Rome or its laws relinquished their right to live and deserved death. This common attitude kept the executions as the midday mainstay of the games up till the end of the imperial age. What is notable is Martial's explicit detail of the execution:

"His mangled limbs lived, though dripping with blood, and his body no longer looked like a body. He had probably been a parricide, or had killed a master, or had despoiled a temple of its secret gold, or had raised the torch of an incendiary to fire Rome. His guilt must have surpassed in enormity anything recorded in the annals of crime; since what was designed for entertainment was converted into a most dreadful punishment."
—Martial, *Epigrams*, translated by Andrew Amos

While members of the plebian class made up the majority of those who stayed for the lunchtime bill, there were also Romans of rank and privilege who couldn't get enough of the executions. Emperors Commodus and Claudius, in particular, were said to take great pleasure from the entertainment, while Nero was responsible for inventing a particularly brutal method of execution called the *tunica molesta*. This dressed the condemned person in a tunic soaked with pitch before they were crucified and then set on fire. Nero executed numbers of Christians this way, which he then used as human torches to illuminate his nighttime spectacles.

Execution *ad flammas* (by flames) was commonly used alongside *ad bestias* (by wild beasts) as a punishment for antisocial crimes, meted out to arsonists, murderers, treasonous slaves, and groups considered to have conspired against Rome, including Christians. Symbolically

Letter to the Romans

Christians were often executed *ad bestias* and *ad gladium* for refusing to recognize the imperial cult that made the reigning emperor a god. The legacy of these Christians as the first martyrs is often still recounted in religious literature of today. One of the most famous martyrs was Ignatius of Antioch, who was sentenced *ad bestias* in the second century CE. Here he describes waiting to be transported to the Colosseum:

"From Syria even unto Rome I fight with beasts, both by land and sea, both by night and day, being bound to ten leopards, I mean a band of soldiers, who, even when they receive benefits, show themselves all the worse. But I am the more instructed by their injuries as a disciple of Christ. May I enjoy the wild beasts that are prepared for me; and I pray they may be found eager to rush upon me, which also I will entice to devour me speedily, and not deal with me as with some, whom, out of fear, they have not touched. But if they be unwilling to assail me, I will compel them to do so. Pardon me in this: I know what is for my benefit. Now I begin to be a disciple. And

Above: A nineteenth-century engraving of Christian martyrs receiving their sentence *ad bestias* in the arena.

let no one, of things visible or invisible, envy me that I should attain to Jesus Christ. Let fire and the cross; let the crowds of wild beasts; let tearings,

breakings and dislocations of bones; let cutting off of members; let shatterings of the whole body; and let all the dreadful torments of the devil come upon me: only let me attain to Jesus Christ."

—Ignatius, *Letter to the Romans*,
translated by Alexander Roberts and James Donaldson

A DAY AT THE GAMES   177

Left: An ivory diptych from the Eastern Roman capital of Constantinople showing a *venatio* from 500 CE. The last recorded gladiatorial animal hunt took place in 536.

the flames and beasts represented the forces of nature that the condemned criminal had exposed themselves to in spurning the protection of the Roman Empire.

The evening before their deaths, condemned criminals would be brought to the amphitheater to spend their last night packed together in the tiny cells of the *hypogeum*. In the morning they were split into two groups—citizens and non-citizens. First to be executed were the citizens, who were normally afforded the privilege of a speedy death. This meant execution *ad gladium* (by the sword), which, in the early imperial age, was decapitation via a sword blow. Later, beheading was reserved for senators, equestrians and other members of the Roman elite. By comparison, lower status citizens began to be sentenced to *ad bestias* as well as *ad gladium* as the days of empire progressed.

Midday Methods

The purpose of the executions in the arena was to make a public show that included humiliation, degradation, and extreme pain for the condemned. Carrying out the executions in public was believed to reinforce Rome's social order and dissuade people from breaking the law—as well as showing everyone the ultimate price for doing so. But it also had to be entertaining, or the crowd would become bored and belligerent. Those spectators who had

stayed for the lunchtime event wanted a show, and it was up to the *editor* to provide one with maximum impact.

To start with, the condemned citizens were led into the arena and decapitated or killed with a single sword thrust. A longer-lasting event would often be introduced straight afterwards. This pitted one condemned citizen armed with a *gladius* against another, unarmed citizen. The armed man would chase and catch the other (or be forced to do so by attendants carrying hot branding irons), and stab him to death. He was then made to hand the *gladius* to the next condemned man entering the arena, who would in turn begin the chase. This continued until the last man standing was finished off by a *venator*.

Then the non-citizens were executed. Often the trapdoor and pulley system of the *hypogeum* were part of the killing apparatus. A man already in the throes of crucifixion, for example, would rise up from the arena floor so that lions and tigers could attack him on his cross. Other people would be tied to chariots that were then wheeled across the arena to the beasts waiting on the other side. Some of the condemned were simply nailed upside down on a cross and left as bait for any interested animal.

A statue found in North Africa shows a woman astride a bull, naked from the waist up with her hands tied behind her back. The bull has fallen to its knees and a leopard is shown mauling the women's chest. This was not the only example of the degradation of women in the arena.

To provide variety to the executions, popular stories from mythology were often reenacted. It was during the reign of Nero that this method of execution became a common feature and the emperor himself often devised new storylines for them. One such story concerned the myth of Daedalus and Icarus, who escaped from the Minotaur's labyrinth by wearing wings made from feathers and wax. However, Icarus's wings melted when he flew too close to the Sun, and he fell into the sea and drowned.

The myth reenacted as an execution had varying degrees of success during Nero's games, as Suetonius recounts: "Icarus at his very first attempt fell close by the imperial couch and bespattered the emperor with his blood."

In a later retelling of the same myth, a criminal was made to play the part of Daedalus. Using wires and a system of winches, Daedalus was then made to fly over the arena so he could be dropped into an enclosure of bears, which devoured him.

Another story popularly played out as an execution was that of the villain Laureolus, a bandit chieftain and common subject of Roman mime. In an account recorded by Martial, a condemned criminal was made to play the part of Laureolus. Laureolus, in this instance, took the form of Prometheus, a Greek titan who was punished for eternity by being tied to a rock and having his liver eaten by an eagle:

Facing page: Christian martyrs pray before an approaching lion in a painting by Jean-Leon Gerome.

"May I enjoy the wild beasts that are prepared for me; and I pray they may be found eager to rush upon me, which also I will entice to devour me speedily."

—*Ignatius*

Right: Christians being tied to stakes and mauled by wild animals is a popular view of martyrs in the amphitheater. However, the Romans went to great pains to provide variety in their executions.

"Like as Prometheus was chained to a rock, whilst a vulture with unassuaged voracity was devouring his vitals, so Laureolus, in the amphitheater, was stretched on a real cross, presenting his heart to be torn by a Caledonian bear."
—Martial, *Epigrams*, translated by Andrew Amos

In this case, the mauling of the criminal playing Laureolus by a Scottish bear while he was nailed to a cross seems to have provided effective entertainment. However, like the *venationes*, the successful staging of such an event was largely dependent on the behavior of the animals. The Roman *editores* were only too aware that tired, frightened, or otherwise reluctant animals could ruin an expensively staged execution. For them, this was just part of the job. However, condemned Christians and those who documented their deaths took the animals unwillingness as a sign of the martyr's innocence. They believed that God allowed the beasts to kill only the guilty.

A famous example was the martyrdom of Perpetua and Felicitas during the reign of Emperor Septimius Severus. Severus had banned imperial subjects from becoming Christians and persecuted those who had done so. In 203 CE, Severus sentenced thousands of Christians to be executed in the amphitheater in Carthage. Among them was

Left: A bear approaches a half-naked Christian in the Colosseum. An animal's unwillingness to kill a Christian martyr was often taken as a sign of their innocence.

newly converted noble women Perpetua and her pregnant servant Felicitas.

Christian tellers of the story of Perpetua and Felicitas emphasized that the women rejected a chance to renounce their faith and instead chose a martyr's death. Felicitas even worried that the impending birth of her child would halt proceedings and delay her martyrdom. However, it is not Perpetua and Felicitas who are spared by the beasts sent to gore them, but a Christian called Saturus sentenced to die alongside them. Saturus was tied to a wild boar that refused to spear him with its tusks and instead dragged him around the arena floor. The boar then charged at an attending *bestiarus* and killed him. A second attempt at execution was made by attaching Saturus to a frame and setting a bear on him. But the bear refused to attack. A successful third attempt had Saturus torn to pieces by a leopard. However, the crowd was so angry with the ineptitude of the *editor* that they demanded Saturus's throat be cut in front of them so they could see that he was dead.

The crowd was also angered when Perpetua and Felicitas had to face the animals. As the naked women were brought into the arena, a disgusted cry went up from the spectators when they saw milk dripping from Felicitas's lactating breasts. The women were sent down to be covered up before being led into arena once more. After being

whipped they were trampled by wild cows, but both survived. Swordsmen were then sent in to finish the women off. It was said that Perpetua had to help her trembling executioner by holding his hand steady so that he could slit her throat.

The Finishing Off

Like the *venatio* that came before, the midday executions ended with an arena littered with corpses. At the end of the executions two men dressed as mythological figures would enter the arena—Charon the ferryman, carrying a two-handled mallet, and the god Mercury, who brandished a long rod of iron with a red-hot end. As the pair walked among the corpses of the dead, Mercury would poke them with his smoldering point and Charon would bash them with his hammer. This ensured that nobody could escape the arena by playing dead.

THE GLADIATORS' GAMES

As the blood and corpses were removed from the arena and fresh sand laid down, the atmosphere was buoyed by those returning from their lunchtime break. The day was designed to build up to the gladiator fights and in the early afternoon the amphitheater was sizzling with excitement.

As spectators took their seats, light entertainment such as mock fights between

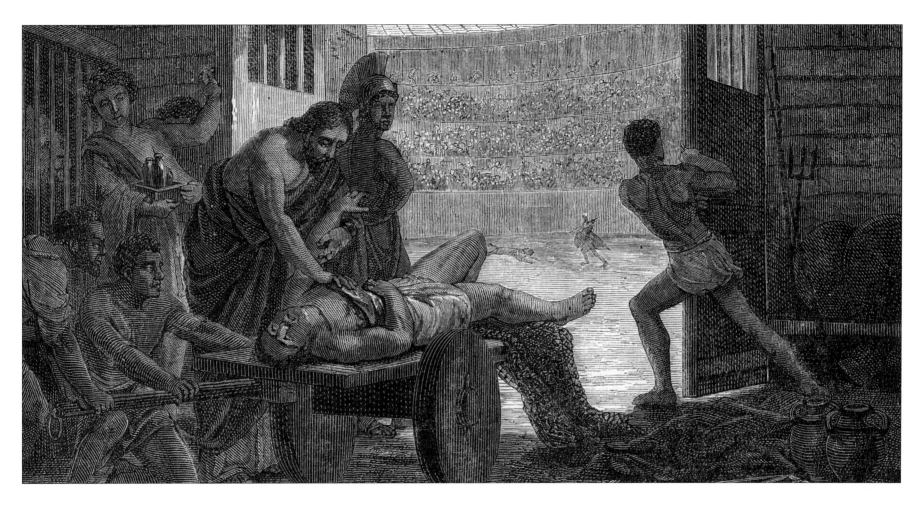

Above: Galen was a famous Roman doctor who studied in Greece and Alexandria before returning to become chief physician in the *ludus* in his home city of Pergamum, Turkey. Here, he tends to a wounded gladiator.

paegniarii often took place. These were gladiator clowns who fought with wooden swords and were usually chosen because they were dwarves or disabled. Another display by two *andabatae*—gladiators who fought blind in a helmet with no eyeholes—also sometimes helped warm up the crowd. Treated as another comic turn, the *andabatae* were led to each other via instructions called out from the spectators. The bout only ended when one had stumbled upon his quarry and killed him.

When everyone had found their seats, the arena was emptied and a hush would fall across the amphitheater. The *pompa*, or opening ceremony,

Above: Galen was a famous Roman doctor who studied in Greece and Alexandria before returning to become chief physician in the *ludus* in his home city of Pergamum, Turkey. Here, he tends to a wounded gladiator.

Above: Gladiators fight en masse in this seventeenth-century artwork. Group gladiatorial battles were occasionally recorded, but they were rare.

Androclus and the Lion

One of the best-known stories of a condemned man being thrown to the lions is that of Androclus, a slave from the time of Augustus. Androclus had been sentenced *ad bestias* in an amphitheater in Rome after escaping his abusive master in Africa. The following account was recorded by writer Aulus Gellius in the second century CE:

> "… during the executions of the slaves, one particular lion impressed the crowd with the huge size of his body, his terrific and deep roar, the development of his muscles and the mane streaming over his shoulders … There was brought in, among many others who had been condemned to fight with the wild beasts, the slave of an ex-consul; the slave's name was Androclus. When that lion saw him from a distance … he stopped short as if in amazement, and then approached the man slowly and quietly, as if he recognized him. Then, wagging his tail in a mild and caressing way, after the manner and fashion of fawning dogs, he came close to the man, who was now half-dead from fright, and gently licked his feet and hands. The man

Right: Androclus is reunited with the lion, his patient and savior.

Androclus, while submitting to the caresses of so fierce a beast, regained his lost courage and gradually turned his eyes to look at the lion … you might have seen man and lion exchange joyful greetings, as if they had recognized each other."

Androclus was called over to Augustus to explain the extraordinary turn of events. He told the emperor he pulled a thorn from the lion's paw when he had been on the run and seeking shelter in his cave. In gratitude, the lion had befriended Androclus and brought him meat to feed on, but Androclus was eventually captured and sentenced to the amphitheater. Augustus promptly granted Androclus and the lion a *missio* and the pair departed together. Aulus describes the happy ending:

> "Afterwards … we used to see Androclus with the lion, attached to a slender leash, making the rounds of the shops throughout the city; Androclus was given money, the lion was sprinkled with flowers and everyone who met them anywhere exclaimed: 'This is the lion that was a man's friend, this is the man who was physician to a lion.'"

—Aulus Gellius, *The Attic Nights*, translated by J.C. Rolfe

Right: The gladiators are led into the amphitheater during a *pompa*. Gladiators also sometimes entered the arena without their armor and weaponry to show off their bodies before the crowd.

was about to begin. The best record of a *pompa* comes from a relief at Pompeii. This shows the front of the solemn procession entering the arena being led by two *lictors* dressed in togas, the official garment of the Roman citizen. The *lictors* were officers of the holder of the games and carried *fasces*, a bundle of sticks wrapped around an axe that acted as an emblem of their power. Walking behind the *lictors* were two trumpeters and four men carrying a *ferculum* on their shoulders. This was a litter used to transport the statues of the Roman deities of warfare such as Hercules, Mars, and Nemesis. The next figures carried a tablet with information about the fights and palm branches for the victors. Behind these figures was the *editor* himself, dressed in a toga and followed by six assistants carrying helmets and shields.

Towards the end of the procession two men led in the horses used by the *equites*, who would begin the afternoon event. With them were more musicians, one carrying trumpet and another a horn. Music was an intrinsic part of the gladiator fights played not only during the *pompa* but also to accompany the contests themselves. Instruments, including tubas, trumpets, flutes, and water organs, were played through the peaks and troughs of combat, much as a modern orchestra did for silent movies.

Above: A bas-relief of parading gladiators with officials in the background.

Entering the Arena

Quintilian was a first-century-CE rhetorician known for his oratory. Here, he describes the plight of a gladiator about to enter the arena. It is interesting to note Quintilian's mention of the red-hot metal plates and rods used to encourage unwilling gladiators into action:

"And now the day was here, and the people had gathered for the spectacle of my punishment and now for show throughout the arena the bodies of those about to perish had led off a procession of their own death. The sponsor (*editor*) was sitting there piling up favor derived from our blood. Although no one could know my fortune, my family, my father, because I was separated from my homeland by the sea, among certain spectators nevertheless one thing made me pitiable, that I seem inadequately prepared; truly I was destined to be a certain victim of the arena, no one had caused less expense for the giver of the games than I; there was noise everywhere produced by the equipment of death; here a sword was being sharpened, there someone was heating metal plates, here rods were produced, there whips. You would have thought that these men were pirates. The trumpets were blaring with their funereal sound, and the funeral procession was proceeding … before anyone had died everywhere there were wounds, moans, gore; one could only see danger."

—Quintilian, *Declamations*, translated by H.E. Butler

Right: A *provocator* or "challenger" was a medium-armed gladiator, who first appeared during the Republican period.

Left: The *galerus* was a shoulder guard used by the *retiarius* gladiator. The metal at the top of the *galerus* was bent away from the gladiator's head, to ensure full mobility.

Far left: A *secutor* helmet, one of the remarkably well-preserved artifacts discovered at Pompeii.

Often the gladiators themselves would have joined the *pompa*, and if not, they would follow into the arena straight afterwards. In a prelude to the actual fighting, this was a chance for the audience to watch the gladiators without their armor or helmets. The gladiators would show off their muscles and prowess by stretching and sparring with each other with wooden or blunted weaponry. With this done, the gladiators were sent below the arena and an inspection of their real weaponry took place. This was specifically to check that the weapons were as lethal as possible. Emperor Commodus was often known to enter the arena personally to ensure the sharpness of the swords.

After the weapons had been inspected the arena would be deserted once more, leaving the crowd waiting for the first pair of dueling gladiators. Trumpeters signalled the start of combat, overseen by a principal referee (*summa rudis*) and his assistant (*secunda rudis*). There were strict rules for the combat, but little is known about them. It is believed that some contests took place within white chalk boundaries. If the gladiators stepped outside of these lines the fight was stopped and the fighters sent back to their starting positions.

"The people had gathered for the pectacle of my punishment and now for show throughout the arena the bodies of those about to perish had led off a procession of their own death."

—*Quintilian*

ΜΑΡΓΑΡΕΙΤΗC   ΕΛΛΗΝΙΚΟC

Below: A rare gladiatorial mosaic from the ancient
Roman city of Kourion, in Cyprus.

Right: An official oversees a contest which has been won by a *thraex* carrying his curved *sica*.

The crowd had a good knowledge of the rules of the contests and an appreciation of the fighting skills displayed by each gladiator. The spectacle was being performed for the pleasure of the spectators, and they would make their feelings clear by shouting, jeering, and cheering loudly through every moment of the bout.

For the gladiators themselves, the long hours of attacking a *palus* and their respective drills with *doctores* would suddenly become matters of life and death. Their training had provided them with a wide variety of moves—lunging, thrusting, and parrying—that they now relied on for their very survival. Blades would hardly ever have crossed, but instead shields were used to repel blows. Shields would also be employed to batter at the opponent, to injure, unarm him, or deprive him of his helmet or armor. Each gladiator would keenly scan for exposed or vulnerable body parts that could be sliced or cut to disable his opponent. As both gladiators circled each other, every last ounce of energy would be conserved for a final, fatal thrust. There were no rounds in a gladiator fight and the combat would go on until one was declared the winner. In longer contests, however, the referee could call for break. In a Pompeian relief, two gladiators are shown resting during such an interval. Assistants are depicted massaging the resting gladiators and serving them drinks.

Right: A Roman clay lamp from the third century features two gladiators in combat.

Facing page: Gladiator doctor Galen tends to a wounded fighter. The medical attention given to gladiators did not extend to many other people of the time.

> "His mangled limbs lived, though dripping with blood, and his body no longer looked like a body."
>
> —Martial

While contemporary sources sing the praises of those gladiators who fought with courage and fortitude, not all combatants were as heroic. Some gladiatorial contests were short, brutal, and involved terrified men trying to escape, refusing to fight, or being easily dispatched by a far greater opponent. In such cases, the referees would goad the fighters with their sticks, or send in assistants brandishing whips, torches, and red-hot irons.

Gladiators were trained to display the Roman virtue, *contemptus mortis*, or contempt of death, and to die with honor. But many gladiator contests were not decided by one killing the other. Instead, these fights ended when one was too exhausted or injured to continue, or had simply been beaten by the other.

In this instance the defeated gladiator would throw away his sword, if he still had one, and raise his index finger in submission. His victorious opponent would then look towards the emperor or *editor* for further instruction: they, in turn would look to the crowd. Now it was up to the spectators to decide if a gladiator had fought honorably enough to live. If the gladiator had fought valiantly according to the Roman *virtus*, then his life was often spared. If the crowd made a united chant of "*mitte*" (let him go) and the emperor agreed, the gladiator would be granted a *missio*, or reprieve, and allowed to leave the arena alive.

If the emperor did not grant a *missio* (Caligula and Domitian reportedly rejected the crowd's wishes at times), then the defeated gladiator was still expected to die with honor. To do this he would wrap his arms around his opponent's legs and allow him to administer the coup de grace between his shoulder blades or into his neck. As this happened the crowd would shout, "*Habet*," or "He has it."

Reliefs and mosaics often show the pivotal moment when one gladiator accepts his deathblow. On a relief from Naples, a defeated gladiator is pictured with his hands around his opponent's knees as this man holds his head and thrusts his sword into his throat. In a relief from Bologna, a defeated gladiator kneels as he awaits to receive his opponent's death blow. In the Borghese estate mosaic, a gladiator is shown plunging his sword into another's back with both hands. In the Zliten mosaic a *hoplomachus* is shown burying his sword in a *murmillo*'s chest, as the *murmillo* clutches at it hopelessly.

With the contest now over, the victor would approach the emperor's box to be rewarded with a laurel wreath and, at times, a purse. He would then wave to cheers and applause from the crowd as he left the arena. His dead opponent would be carried out on a covered stretcher to the amphitheater mortuary, where gladiators' throats were routinely cut to ensure they were dead. The corpse was then stripped of his weapons and armor, which would be recycled at the *ludus*, and sent to whatever burial his *collegia* had organized.

The Long Day Closes

Gladiator fights were often fast and ferocious and lasted for 10 to 15 minutes. There were of course exceptions to this—some contests could end in a few brutal and bloody minutes, while other bouts between evenly matched opponents lasted for hours. There is a famous example of just such an epic contest taking place during the Colosseum's inauguration. The two gladiators involved were the Gallic slave Priscus and a free man, Versus. Their story is described by Martial:

"As Priscus and Versus each drew out the contest and the struggle between the pair long stood equal, shouts loud and often sought discharge for the combatants. But Titus obeyed his own law (the law was that the bout go on without shield until a finger be raised). What he could do, he did, often giving dishes and presents. But an end to the even strife was found: equal they fought, equal they yielded. To both Titus sent wooden swords and to both palms. Thus valor and skill had their reward. This has happened under no prince but you, Caesar: two fought and both won."

—Martial, *Epigrams*, translated by D.R. Shackleton Bailey

Martial's gushing tone probably reflects the good feeling in the crowd caused by the emperor's decision—allowing both gladiators to leave the arena as free men.

It was the great desire of the emperor or *editor* of the games to send home the spectators satisfied at the end of the day. Caesar's bread and circuses regime, after all, was designed to prevent the people turning on their emperor. Emperor Titus came up with a special crowd-pleasing finale to round off a long day at the amphitheater. Cassius Dio explains:

"He would throw down into the theater from aloft little wooden balls variously inscribed, one designating some article of food, another clothing, another a silver vessel or perhaps a gold one, or again horses, pack-animals, cattle, or slaves. Those who seized them were to carry them to the dispensers of the bounty, from whom they would receive the article named."

—Cassius Dio, *Roman History*, translated by Earnest Cary

The practice of handing out gifts at the end of the gladiatorial games continued under Domitian and became an institutionalized aspect of the spectacles. With the love of his people purchased through handouts of grain, an extravagant day of gladiatorial combat and free gifts, an emperor could rest easy. For the spectators, on the other hand, the day resembled any other spent watching the games. There were moments both memorable and forgettable, but most importantly, more games were to follow tomorrow, and the next day and for several more days running. Spectacles of the imperial period were long indeed: Trajan's games following his triumph in Dacia ran for 123 days in a row and featured contests between 10,000 gladiators. The emperors made sure they spared no expense in buying the goodwill of their subjects.

Facing page: The stadium of Domitian was used by gladiators after fire damaged the Colosseum in 217 CE. The Christian martyr St. Agnes was executed there aged 13 during the reign of Diocletian.

"As Priscus and Versus each drew out the contest and the struggle between the pair long stood equal, shouts loud and often sought discharge for the combatants."

—*Martial*

The Decline of the Games

By the mid-third century CE, the Roman Empire was beginning to come undone. Rome's frontiers were under increasing attack from Barbarian tribes, Goths, and Persians, and its army was draining the imperial coffers to stem the tide. There was little money left to hold large, lavish gladiatorial contests. But Rome was also under attack from a more pernicious foe: Christianity.

Rome's reaction to the rolling numbers of assaults on its borders—which included Gothic invasions in Greece and Asia Minor, and the Franks in Sicily and North Africa—was to install new emperors. In total, 49 different emperors were enthroned between 239 and 285 CE during vain and desperate bids to find a savior. The army was now Rome's most important asset, and the legions themselves often hand-picked the emperors. Predictably, these rulers were usually military commanders who would march with their men at the head of the line.

Facing page: The Colosseum in Rome has been a popular tourist attraction for hundreds of years; millions still flock there annually. The underground *hypogeum* can be clearly seen beneath the arena floor.

Right: *Portrait of the Four Tetrarchs* is a sculpture of the four Roman emperors under Diocletian's Tetrachy.

One such emperor was Diocletian, son of a Balkan peasant farmer whose skill and acumen had seen him rise rapidly through the military ranks. Diocletian had no interest in the traditions of Rome or the outdated model of an emperor as first citizen. Instead, he ruled like an omnipotent god; his subjects were expected to prostrate themselves in his presence and, if lucky, kiss the purple hem of his toga. To ensure a direct line of command below him, Diocletian split the empire into four parts, called the Tetrarchy, and initiated bureaucratic reforms. These reforms took administrative powers away from the provincial elites and put it into the hands of a new centralized system.

Rome's reliance on the elite members of its provincial territories had grown thin. The towns and cities at Rome's farthest reaches were slipping from the empire's grasp, and the capital could no longer depend on them for income. There was also a new spiritual movement making an appearance

Right: A twentieth-century illustration of the 410 CE sacking of Rome by Alaric and his Visigoth army.

Facing page: An illustration of Nero's persecution of the Christian saints Peter and Paul.

> *"We order that there may be no more gladiator combats. Those who were condemned to become gladiators for their crimes are to work from now on in the mines."*
>
> —Constantine

in far-flung Roman territories: Christianity. This alternative to the materialistic ideology meted out by Rome became popular with rich and poor alike.

Religious Freedom and the Fall of Rome
For centuries, local aristocratic families had worked as Rome's provincial administrators and kept the colonial machinery of empire ticking over. They maintained the *pax romana*, collected taxes, provided men for the army, and, most importantly

of all, made sure every local inhabitant paid their respects to the imperial cult. Part of this allegiance included the giving of gladiatorial games in the emperor's honor. In return, provincial citizens were left alone to do and believe whatever they liked. Rome had no interest in proscribing religious practices. As a pagan civilization it allowed the worship of any and all foreign gods. But Rome's reluctance to offer spiritual guidance was to be a great contributor to the fall of the empire.

While many provinces had prospered under the *pax romana*, there was clearly something rotten at the heart of Rome. The scandalous sadism of emperors such as Nero, Caligula, and Commodus must have swept through the empire's provinces like wildfire. So did news about the opponents of imperial rule that had ended up performing as gladiators or being executed en masse in the arena.

> *"Though you drag my body to that place and set me down there, you cannot force me to give my mind or lend my eyes to these shows."*
>
> —*Saint Augustine*

Persecution against Christians was never a coherent policy, but it continued in stops and starts for centuries under different emperors. Nero scapegoated Christians for the 64 CE burning of Rome and had thousands burned alive to illuminate his games. In 70 CE, Titus sacked Jerusalem in a brutal suppression of the Jewish revolt there. Tens of thousands of Jews were executed in amphitheaters or used as slave labor to build the Colosseum.

Facing page: A seventeenth-century painting of Emperor Titus ordering the destruction of the Temple of Jerusalem, after his siege on the city. A triumph and gladiatorial games celebrated the victory.

Right: The arch of Septimius Severus in the Roman city of Leptis Magna, Libya. Severus was a local boy who went on to become emperor of Rome.

Titus famously constructed a triumphant arch to commemorate his victory, but it became a monument to the beginning of the end of Rome as Titus knew it.

Those Jews dispossessed from Jerusalem now spread far and wide across the Mediterranean. With them they took their belief in the messianic cult that would become Christianity. As the religion took root, Roman emperors periodically ordered the persecution of Christians to try and suppress this burgeoning new force.

One such persecution came in 203 CE under Septimius Severus. Severus ordered the massacre of thousands of Christians in the amphitheater in Carthage, which included the noblewoman Perpetua and her servant Felicitas. The story behind the executions that turned both women into saints introduced a new term into the Roman lexicon: martyr.

Perpetua came from exactly the kind of elite provincial family that would have been responsible for the administration of the Roman Empire in its colonies. Instead of the material wealth and free enterprise offered by Rome, Christianity

Facing page: An eighteenth-century etching of Christian persecutions under Emperor Diocletian in the early third century CE. These failed to bring Christians back to traditional Roman religion.

Right: Constantine was the first Roman emperor to convert to Christianity. Christian emperors eventually abolished the gladiatorial games.

provided spiritual enrichment to those looking beyond the baths, aqueducts, and amphitheaters of empire. Choosing the religion made sense for those provincial plebeians who were already under the heel of Rome. But it was not until Christianity permeated the ranks of the ruling classes that it really began to take hold.

The Conversion of Empire

By 303 CE, Christianity had made serious inroads into the aristocracy of the Roman capital itself. As a result Diocletian brought about his "Great Persecution," ordering that all Christian scriptures and places of worship be destroyed, and that any equestrian, senator, or other patrician found guilty of practicing the religion be stripped of their rank and privileges. All Christians across the empire would lose their legal rights under the emperor's persecution. While Diocletian made it clear he wanted the worship of Roman traditional gods to continue, his attempted suppression of Christianity only served to make it stronger. The problem for the Romans was that Christians considered martyrdom to be an honor and not a punishment, as it ensured

their place in heaven. The tales of those martyrs killed in the amphitheater spread far and wide across the empire and were read out at Christian gatherings.

While Rome and its pagan gods may have tolerated the gods of its conquered subjects, Christians were not so open-minded. For them there was only one God. As the numbers of Romans converting to Christianity grew, it was only a matter of time before an emperor also became one. This was Constantine, who famously claimed to have converted to Christianity after seeing a cross in the sky on the day he defeated his rival, Maxentius. Maxentius was one of the emperors of the Tetrarchy who had declared war on Constantine. With Maxentius killed, Constantine was able to dissolve the failed Tetrarchy and once again unite the empire under one emperor. His reign would signal the rise of Christianity as the dominant religion of the ancient world.

It would also end the period of imperial Rome as the world had known it and usher in a new epoch of Roman history, one that was based around its new capital city of Constantinople, today's Istanbul. The gradual conversion of Rome from a pagan empire to a Christian one would spell the beginning of the end for the gladiatorial games.

In 313 CE, Constantine issued an imperial edict for toleration of Christianity across the empire, and in 325 CE he invited bishops into his inner circle of advisors. In the same year he issued another edict, this time to Maximus, a governor from the eastern provinces, banning gladiator fights:

Left: A relief of a gladiator from a Roman sarcophagus, Turkey.

Facing page: The theater of the ancient city of Hierapolis, Turkey. Gladiatorial contests continued throughout Rome's eastern provinces in the fourth century despite Constantine's edict banning them.

"In times in which peace and peace relating to domestic affairs prevail bloody demonstrations displease us. Therefore, we order that there may be no more gladiator combats. Those who were condemned to become gladiators for their crimes are to work from now on in the mines. Thus they pay for their crimes without having to pour their blood."
—*Codex Theodosianus* 15.12.1

Despite Constantine's edict, gladiatorial games continued throughout his reign. In 328 CE, a spectacle was held in the ancient city of Antioch, near the modern city of Antakya, Turkey. Similar spectacles followed in other eastern cities. However, the bishops of these cities decreed that no Christian would be allowed to work in the amphitheaters and no gladiator performing in them could be baptized.

The Christian aversion to the spectacles was partly to do with the persecution of Christians and their subsequent end in the arena. However, there was a more important point about the games that also did not fit with Christian ideals. This was to do with the *infamis*, the disgraced, being given a chance to redeem himself in the arena. A gladiator could win his salvation by displaying Roman *virtus*—bravery, courage, contempt for death—and be granted his life by the emperor. But in the Christian world only God could offer this salvation, and he did not grant it as a reward for prowess with a sword. The emperor's position as granter of life and liberty was one of many reasons the church would eventually break with him altogether and become its own institution of power, ruled over by a pope.

The Corrupting Contests

The Christian view on the games was that encouraging the enjoyment of combat and public executions turned otherwise moral men into savages. This sentiment is described by Saint Augustine, who tells the story of his friend Alypius and his reluctant visit to the games:

"He had gone on to Rome … and there he was carried away again with an incredible passion for the gladiatorial shows. For, although he had been utterly opposed to such spectacles and detested them, one day he met by chance a company of his acquaintances and fellow students returning from dinner; and, with a friendly violence, they drew him, resisting and objecting vehemently, into the amphitheater, on a day of those cruel and murderous shows.

"He protested to them: 'Though you drag my body to that place and set me down there, you cannot force me to give my mind or lend my eyes to these shows. Thus I will be absent while present, and so overcome both you and them.' When they heard this, they dragged him on in … But Alypius kept his eyes closed and forbade his mind to roam abroad after such wickedness. Would that he had shut his ears also! For when one of the combatants fell in the fight, a mighty cry from the whole audience stirred him so strongly that, overcome by curiosity and still prepared (as he thought) to despise and rise superior to it no matter what it was, he opened his eyes and was struck with a

Above: A *retiarius* and *murmillo* in combat.

deeper wound in his soul than the victim whom he desired to see had been in his body … For, as soon as he saw the blood, he drank in with it a savage temper, and he did not turn away, but fixed his eyes on the bloody pastime, unwittingly drinking in the madness—delighted with the wicked contest and drunk with blood lust. "He was now no longer the same man who came in, but was one of the mob he came into, a true companion of those who had brought him thither. Why need I say more? He

looked, he shouted, he was excited, and he took away with him the madness that would stimulate him to come again: not only with those who first enticed him, but even without them; indeed, dragging in others besides."

—Saint Augustine, *Confessions and Enchiridion*, translated by Albert C. Outler

In the fourth century, instances of the gladiatorial games diminished under the Christian emperors who came directly after Constantine. However, none seemed interested in abolishing them altogether. The spectacles held by Constantine's sons from 333–337 CE are shown in lavish detail in the Galleria Borghese mosaic, which decorated the floor of a large villa near the Colosseum. The Philocalian Calendar, an illustrated codex of the year 354 CE, shows days

---

"He [Telemachus] went himself into the stadium, and stepping down into the arena, endeavoured to stop the men who were wielding their weapons against one another."

—*Theodoret of Cyrus*

set aside for both chariot races and gladiatorial games. However, while chariot races took place on 64 of these days, gladiatorial contests occurred on only 10. This was a far cry from the weeks-long spectacles that took place at the height of empire,

and a telling sign of the lack of imperial funds still available for such events.

The last decades of the games saw a confused and changeable imperial line. In 367 CE, Valentinianus I banned Christians from being sentenced to the arena, but allowed non-Christians to be punished in this way. Emperor Theodosius I abolished heathen festivals, but in 393 CE the senator Symmachus, bent on restoring the pagan traditions of Rome, was allowed to hold a spectacle in the capital.

Above: Russell Crowe plays Maximus, a fictional Roman general turned gladiator in the movie *Gladiator*. Despite its great box office success, *Gladiator* was heavily criticized for its many historical inaccuracies.

Left: Telemachus the Monk traveled to Rome in 404 CE to try and stop the gladiatorial games. His protest was not received well.

Facing page: A relief from Turkey of a *venatio*. Although gladiator contests had been banned, fights between men and beasts continued in the eastern provinces throughout the fifth century CE.

Theodosius's successor, Honorius, closed down all *ludi* in Rome in 399 CE, but did not ban the games themselves.

Instead it was an incident in 404 CE that sounded the death knell for the gladiatorial games. Earlier, a monk called Telemachus had traveled from the empire's eastern provinces to Rome to protest against the gladiator fights. During one performance, he left his seat to intervene in a contest between two gladiators, who were ordered to tear the monk limb from limb. Horrified by the news, Honorius banned the games in the capital for good.

Honorius's ban was not the end for the spectacles—games continued to be held into the 440s—but their power to attract spectators had waned. There were several reasons for this. First, the money set aside for imperial games had all but disappeared. This meant that the games presented were short and provided few gladiators for the public's entertainment. Those attending the amphitheaters would often have left disappointed. Second, the numbers of spectators dwindled as more and more of the population became practicing

Christians, and Christian leaders made sure their flocks stayed away from the spectacles. Third, Rome fell in 410 CE to Alaric, a Visigoth King who sacked the city. Rome continued after this under its last western emperor, Romulus Augustulus, but he was deposed in 476 CE by Odovacar, a Germanic prince who became King of Italy. The Western Roman Empire and the gladiatorial spectacles it held to display its wealth, power and dominion over its conquered people were now defunct.

Games considered suitable for the Christian crowds continued in the eastern Roman capital of Constantinople throughout the fifth century. These included chariot races, *venationes,* and fights between men and animals. Although contests between gladiators were deemed un-Christian, there were no such issues with the slaughter of animals. *Venationes* carried on into the next century—a spectacle held in 506 CE to celebrate the consulship of Areobindus featured bear baiting and *venatores* hunting lions with spears. Animal hunts continued in the sixth century, although fights between animals and men were banned. The last recorded spectacle involving the hunting of animals was held by Emperor Justinian in 536 CE. After that, even this element of the gladiatorial games faded from view. The Roman spectacles had run their course.

The Decline of the Colosseum

The city of Rome in the fifth century tottered along unstably as its inhabitants faced various Gothic attacks and a great decline in income from the imperial provinces. As the Western empire declined,

the taxes Rome had relied upon dried up. The days of bread and circuses were now well and truly over. The population of Rome dropped steadily as thousands of people left the city. At the beginning of the fifth-century Rome was home to 800,000 inhabitants; by the middle of the sixth century this had dropped to 30,000.

Those who stayed bore witness to the city's atrophy: buildings that had not been destroyed by invading Goths crumbled and collapsed; marble and stone was torn from great classical structures to be used elsewhere; and the statues of emperors were pulled down to make way for churches.

The last recorded *venatio* in the Colosseum was in 519 CE under the Ostrogoth King Theodoric. An account of the games said spectators were astonished by the wild animals brought in from Africa, indicating that no such event had been staged there for years. After that, the building fell into centuries of disrepair. Its sewage system broke down and the *hypogeum* flooded, earthquakes brought down entire exterior walls and the arena floor became an overgrown mound of rubble and weeds. After a while the city's undesirables sought shelter beneath the Colosseum's arches: thieves, beggars, and the homeless. Then, sellers set up small shops and workshops in the passageways below the seating areas. The Colosseum became the place to go to find a blacksmith or cobbler.

By the early Middle Ages the amphitheater had become a site of worship for visiting pilgrims. Written guides from this period incorrectly refer to the pagan Colosseum previously being covered with

Facing page: Ostrogoth Theodoric the Great was the ruler of Italy between 493 and 526 CE. Here he is depicted entering Rome.

"Emperor Honorius in Ravenna received the message from one of the eunuchs, evidently a keeper of the poultry, that Roma had perished. And he cried out, 'And yet it has just eaten from my hands!' For he had a very large cockerel, Roma by name."

—*Procopius*

Above: Nineteenth-century English poet Lord Byron, pictured here, was one of many celebrity visitors to Rome's most famous amphitheater, about which he composed the poem "The Coliseum."

Facing page: An artist's impression of the crumbling Colosseum during the days of its long decay in the Middle Ages. In the nineteenth century the long process of restoration began.

fifteenth century by a burst of new church building in Rome, largely created from the marble, stone and iron plundered from the Colosseum by the wagonload. City planners seemed to want to wipe out every trace of pagan Rome and replace it with a Christian one.

In 1749, Pope Benedict XIV made the Colosseum an official memorial to Christian martyrs and erected a cross in the middle of the arena floor in their honor. Visiting pilgrims then planted their own crosses around the interior of the amphitheater and devout hermits even camped there to protect the now holy site. Other visitors included rich young Europeans in the eighteenth and nineteenth centuries, traveling to Rome as part of the Grand Tour. Some reported their disappointment at finding the Colosseum a site for Christian propaganda.

In 1874, church control over the Colosseum ended when the structure was presented to archeologists by the Italian government. Their investigations began with the removal of the crosses and other religious iconography that had been left there over the decades. Despite heavy protests from the church, the archeologists were able to excavate the *hypogeum* and rubble filling the arena to return the walls, passageways and cells of the Colosseum to their original form. Since then, generations of archeologists and historians have investigated the Colosseum. Their work has enabled us to take an informed view of this crowning glory of the gladiatorial games and its place within the Roman Empire.

a dome of gold and housing a massive gold statue of Apollo. In the eleventh and twelfth centuries, the Normans invaded Italy and the terrified elite families of Rome took shelter in the last of the city's fortified buildings. The Frangipani family occupied the Colosseum and the area around it until 1312. Then, two decades later, an amazing event occurred—a bullfight was organized to celebrate the visit of King Louis of Bavaria. It was the last time blood was spilt on the arena floor for entertainment.

In 1349, another earthquake further damaged the Colosseum and the homeless and peddlers returned to occupy it. They were followed in the

Glossary

ad bestias Execution by being thrown to wild animals.

ad flammas A sentence of execution by being burned alive.

ad gladium A sentence of execution by the sword.

amphitheater Elliptical-shaped building in which the gladiator games were held.

andabatae Novelty gladiators who fought blind wearing helmets without eyeholes and were directed by the crowd during their combat.

armaturae Categories of gladiators.

Baiae Seaside resort on the Bay of Naples for wealthy Romans.

balteus A broad leather gladiator belt.

caestus A boxing glove made from leather straps often reinforced with metal knuckledusters or spikes.

Campus Martius The public area of the ancient Roman capital around two square kilometres in size.

cena libera A banquet held the evening before a spectacle for those performing in it.

collegia A union of gladiators from a particular *ludus* formed to look after each other's rights, such as burials.

compositio The particular pairing of two gladiators to fight each other in the arena.

consul The highest-ranking magistrate of Rome who acted as head of state. Two consuls were in office at any one time and elected for one year only.

crupellarius A rare, extremely heavily-armed gladiator.

dimachaerus A rare gladiator who fought with two swords, one of which was curved.

doctor (pl **doctores**) Gladiator instructor, usually specializing in a particular gladiator category, i.e. a *retiarius* was trained by *doctores retiarii*.

edicta muneris A wall poster that advertised a forthcoming gladiator spectacle.

editor (pl *editores*) The organizer of a spectacle.

eques (pl *equites*) A gladiator who fought on horseback with a spear and then with a sword on foot.

equestrian Also called knights, a social class of wealthy land-owning Romans who, unlike Senators, were able to participate in commerce and finance.

essedarius A rare gladiator who fought from a chariot.

familia gladiatoria The name of a troupe of gladiator often taken from their *lanista* or *ludus* owner.

ferculum A platform used to carry statues of the gods.

First Triumvirate A political alliance formed between Gaius Julius Caesar, Gnaeus Pompeius Magnus (Pompey the Great) and Marcus Licinius Crassus.

forum Centrally-located public meeting place in a Roman city, usually surrounded by public buildings and colonnades.

galerus The shoulder guard worn by the *retiarius*.

gallus An early type of gladiator based on the Gaulish warrior.

habet "He has it!" as shouted out by the crowd when a gladiator has received a deathblow.

hoplomachus A heavily-armed gladiator who fought with a spear and sword.

hypogeum An area underneath the arena floor that contained cells, cages, passageways, and sometimes a series of pulleys, lifts and trapdoors leading into arena.

infamis A disgraced person without legal or social standing.

lanista The owner or manager of a gladiator school responsible for the training and organization of gladiators.

libellus munerarius A detailed program of a gladiatorial spectacle.

lictor A magistrate's attendant and bodyguard who carried the *fasces*, a bundle of sticks wrapped around an axe that acted as an emblem of their power.

ludus (pl *ludi*) 1) A festival held in honor of a diety, such as the *ludi romani*. 2) A gladiator school, such as the *ludus magnus*.

missio Reprieve for a gladiator who had fought bravely enough to retain his life.

munus (pl *munera*) Gladiatorial contests originally held at funerals.

novicius An aspiring gladiatorial recruit.

paegniarius Novelty gladiator who fought with wooden weapons as light entertainment.

palus A pole used for practicing against with a sword.

parma equestris The small shield used by *eques* gladiators and the Roman cavalry.

patrician The wealthy privileged Roman class, which often made up the ranks of the Senate.

plebian Ordinary members of the Roman citizenry.

pollice verso The turning of the thumbs (either up or down) by the crowd to indicate whether a defeated gladiator should be killed or spared.

pompa A procession of gladiators at the beginning of a munus.

princeps "First," a title used by Augustus and the emperors that followed him to describe their imperial position.

provocator A medium-armed gladiator who fought with a breastplate and a *gladius*.

pugio Dagger.

quindecemvir A college of 15 men charged with taking care of the Sibylline books, a collection of oracular utterances in Greek verse that was consulted at times of national crisis.

retiarius Lightly-armed gladiator who fought with a net and trident.

rudiarius A gladiator who has been given a wooden *rudis* and granted his freedom.

rudis A wooden practice sword.

sagittarius Mounted gladiator who fought with a bow.

samnis The oldest type of gladiator modelled on the warrior of the Samnite people.

Second Triumvirate The political alliance of Marcus Aemilius Lepidus, Mark Antony and Octavian (later called Augustus).

secutor Heavily-armed gladiators who wore a helmet with small eyeholes and traditionally fought the *retiarius*.

senate Governing and advisory council made up of patricians.

summa rudis The principal referee in the gladiatorial arena, accompanied by a *secunda rudis*—his assistant.

taurocentae Roman bullfighters.

thraex A heavily-armed gladiator based on the Thracian warrior.

venationes Animal hunts carried out by a type of gladiator called a *venator*.

veteranus A gladiator who had won at least one of his duels in the arena.

Further Information

Books

Futrell, Alison. *The Roman Games.* Historical Sources in Translation. Hoboken, NJ: Wiley-Blackwell, 2006.

Kerrigan, Michael. *The Untold History of the Roman Emperors.* History Exposed. New York: Cavendish Square Publishing, 2017.

Köhne, Eckart, and Cornelia Ewigleben. *Gladiators and Caesars: The Power of Spectacle in Ancient Rome.* Berkley, CA: University of California Press, 2000.

Schiavone, Aldo. *Spartacus.* Revealing Antiquity. Jeremy Carden, trans. Cambridge, MA: Harvard University Press, 2013.

Websites

Gladiator

www.ancient.eu/gladiator

The Ancient History Encyclopedia page on Gladiators details their origins, fighting methods, weapons, and place in Roman society. Other resources include a timeline, photos, and related links.

Gladiators

www.pbs.org/empires/romans/empire/gladiators.html

The PBS article on Gladiators is part of a whole collection of articles and resources on life in the Roman Empire and includes links to key figures.

Gladiators

www.tribunesandtriumphs.org/gladiators

This site has a host of links to information regarding the gladiators. It breaks down the statistics of the different types of gladiators, summarizes popular depictions in film, and has information about gladiator weapons and armor.

Bibliography

Auguet, Roland. *Cruelty and Civilization: The Roman Games*. Abingdon-on-Thames, UK: Routledge, 2012.

Baker, Alan. *The Gladiator: The Secret History of Rome's Warrior Slaves*. London: Ebury Press, 2000.

Balsdon, J.P.V.D. *Life and Leisure in Ancient Rome*. London: Weidenfeld & Nicolson, 2002.

Barton, Carlin A. *The Sorrows of the Ancient Romans: The Gladiator and the Monster*. Princeton, NJ: Princeton University Press, 1995.

Bomgardner, David L. *The Story of the Roman Amphitheatre*. Abingdon-on-Thames, UK: Routledge, 2002.

Bradley, Keith R. *Slavery and Rebellion in the Roman World 140 B.C.–70 B.C.* Bloomington: Indiana University Press, 1998.

Cameron, Alan. *Bread and Circuses: The Roman Emperor and his People*. London: King's College, 1974.

Cassius Dio. *Roman History*. Ian Scott-Kilvert, trans. New York: Penguin Books, 1987.

Claudian. *Works*. Cambridge, MA: Loeb Classical Library, 1989.

Cicero. *Political Speeches*. Oxford World's Classics. D. H. Berry, trans. New York: Oxford University Press, 2009.

Fox, Robin Lane. *Pagans and Christians: In the Mediterranean World from the Second Century AD to the Conversion of Constantine*. New York: Penguin Books, 2006.

Grant, Michael. *The Gladiators*. Harmondsworth, UK: Harmondsworth, 1971.

Harris, William V. *War and Imperialism in Republican Rome 327–70 B.C.* New York: Oxford University Press, 1985.

Hopkins, Keith, and Mary Beard. *The Colosseum*. London: Profile Books, 2011.

Hornblower, Simon, Antony Spawforth, and Esther Eidinow. *The Oxford Classical Dictionary*. New York: Oxford University Press, 2012.

Juvenal. *The Satires*. Oxford World's Classics. New York: Oxford Paperbacks, 2008.

Kohne, Eckart, and Cornelia Ewigleben. *Gladiators and Caesars: The Power of Spectacle in Ancient Rome*. Berkley: University of California Press, 2000.

Kyle, Donald G. *Spectacles of Death in Ancient Rome*. Abingdon-on-Thames, UK: Routledge, 1998.

Livy. *The History of Rome*. New York: Penguin Books, 2002.

Macmullen, Ramsay. *Corruption and the Decline of Rome*. New Haven, CT: Yale University Press, 2002.

Mahoney, Anne. *Roman Sports and Spectacles: A Sourcebook*. Cambridge, MA: Focus Publishing, 2001.

Martial. *Epigrams*. Cambridge, MA: Loeb Classical Library, 1994.

———. *Liber Spectaculorum*. New York: Oxford University Press, 2006.

Meijer, Fik. *Gladiators: History's Most Deadly Sport*. London: Souvenir Press Ltd, 2004.

Nossov, Konstantin. *Gladiator: Rome's Bloody Spectacle*. Oxford, UK: Osprey, 2009.

Petronius. *The Satyricon*. New York: Penguin Books, 1986.

Plass, Paul. *The Game of Death in Ancient Rome: Arena Sport and Political Suicide*. Madison, WI: University of Wisconsin Press, 1999.

Pliny. *Natural History*. New York: Penguin Books, 1991.

Plutarch. *Fall of the Roman Republic*. New York: Penguin Books, 2006.

Poliakoff, Michael B. *Combat Sports in the Ancient World: Competition, Violence, and Culture*. New Haven, CT: Yale University Press, 1995.

Seneca. *Complete Works of Seneca*. Hastings, UK: Delphi Classics, 2014.

Suetonius. *The Twelve Caesars*. New York: Penguin Books, 2007.

Tacitus. *The Annals of Imperial Rome*. New York: Penguin Books, 2012.

Tertullian. *Apology and De Spectaculis*. Cambridge, MA: Loeb Classical Library, 1931.

Wiedemann, Thomas. *Emperors and Gladiators*. Abingdon-on-Thames, UK: Routledge, 1995.

Woodward, Christopher. *In Ruins*. New York: Vintage, 2002.

Selected Roman Emperors: Dates of Rule

Augustus (reigned 27 BCE—14 CE)
Tiberius (reigned 14–37 CE)
Caligula (reigned 37–41 CE)
Claudius (reigned 41–54 CE)
Nero (reigned 54–68 CE)
Trajan (reigned 98–117 CE)
Hadrian (reigned 117–138 CE)

Marcus Aurelius (reigned 161–180 CE)
Commodus (reigned 180–192 CE)
Titus (reigned 79–81 CE)
Domitian (reigned 81–96 CE)
Septimius Severus (reigned 193–211 CE)
Vespasian (reigned 69–79 CE)

Probus (reigned 276–282 CE)
Diocletian (reigned 284–305 CE)
Constantine (reigned 306–337 CE)
Maxentius (ruled as co-emperor, 306–312 CE)
Valentinianus I (reigned 364–375 CE)
Theodosius I (reigned 379–395 CE)

Honorius (reigned 395–423 CE)
Justinian (reigned 527–565 CE)
Romulus Augustulus (reigned October 475—September 4, 476 CE)

Index